Endorsements

"From his years as a college athlete and coach, Wayne Mazzoni has developed a process which gets athletes the results they want."
–Paul Mainieri, Head Baseball Coach, University of Notre Dame

"Help is here for those seeking college scholarships."
–Sport Magazine

"Cort signed with Hawaii last night. It was a difficult decision, and he is very happy with his choice. At the end he had to choose between Loyola Marymount, Utah, Cal-State Fullerton and Hawaii. I am very happy for him and wanted to thank you for the help and advice you have given us over the past year and a half."
–Brett Wilson

"Andy received $16,000 from Monmouth. It's funny—you recommended them from the start. Good call, he likes the school first and playing ball second."
–Tom Mattus

"Lafayette offered Eric $22,000. We need to let the coach know by next Monday to guarantee the money. JMU is now interested. He will have a preliminary offer on Wednesday."
–George Fleckenstein

"Alex was offered $13,000 from Iona. Needless to say, I am pretty happy to save $52,000 over four years. As far as investments go, yours was the best I ever made."
–Joe Giannini

"The type of information Wayne Mazzoni teaches makes me wish I was in high school again. If I knew then, what he has taught me, college would have been a lot cheaper"
–Chris Michalopoulos, Former Univ. of Hartford, Women's Basketball

"Unfortunately high school coaches and guidance counselors don't have the time to help the players like we want to. This is why Wayne's advice is really the most important thing to a high school athlete. It teaches them what to do for themselves to play at the next level. And, all coaches love a player who does things for himself."
–Kip Lukralle, Head Football Coach, Northport High School

"The high school athlete must understand that opportunities are limited at the college level. Those who have the talent must also have the desire and knowledge to make it. Wayne provides that knowledge."
–Andy Baylock, Head Baseball Coach, UConn

"Let me take this opportunity to offer you our thanks for your contribution to the National College Fair. The seminar you presented was right on target and the most well attended of the workshops. We received a lot of very positive feedback from both parents and students. I hope you will be back again next fall."
–Joan Kemnitzer, Guidance Counselor (Elmont Memorial High School), and Board of Directors for NACAC Long Island College Fair

"This is an opportunity for high school kids to take advantage of the expert advice of a professional to better themselves and reach their college dreams. People think college coaches are going to find them, that isn't the case."
–Joe Bonanto, Football Coach, Shelton HS

"Wayne's information goes way beyond expectations. I see parents and athletes so confused about the process, yet after learning from Wayne they knew they were going to play at the college level."
–Harry Efstas, Grand Slam U.S.A.

"Finding out the many techniques to attract coaches made it clear what I have to do to play college sports."
–Ryan Casey, Athlete, Wilton HS

"This book will be a valuable help to high school players and their parents in the quest for obtaining an athletic scholarship."
–Collegiate Baseball

"Wayne Mazzoni, former player and coach at the college level, sheds light on what needs to be done to get to the next level. A must read for every high school athlete and parent."
–WFAN Sports Radio 660 New York

"Wayne Mazzoni is the recruiting guru."
–News 12 New Jersey

"Thank you for all your time, effort, and outstanding presentation at this years DAANJ workshop. Your presentation was organized, interesting, informative, and

well received by those in attendance. I can't thank you enough for all of your assistance, and hard work in preparing and delivering your presentation."
–Thomas Procopio, President,
Directors of Athletic Association of New Jersey

"Wayne Mazzoni has put together all the information one could ever need on the recruiting process. This should be required studying for all student-athletes and parents."
–Ed Blankmeyer, Head Baseball Coach, St. John's

"Thank you for participating in our big event last week in Castleton. Your efforts resulted in wonderfully informative discussions. You did a terrific job of covering the myriad of issues that face high school athletes in the admission and recruiting process. The session evaluation forms were highly favorable."
–Melissa Aborn, College Counselor and staff member of
New England Association of College Admissions Counselors

"The foremost expert on college athletic recruiting."
–Fox Good Day New York

"I wish I had this when I was in high school, I might have played in college instead of keeping the books."
–Sports Fan National Radio

"I can't see how anyone could move to the next level without Wayne's information."
–Empire Sports Network

"Can I keep this copy for my son?"
–News 12 Long Island

"Former college coach, Wayne Mazzoni, helps athletes sort through the confusing recruiting process."
–U.S. News & World Report
"Hey, don't be dumb. Buy it, use it, and have yourself a college career."
–One on One Sports Radio

"After all the work, we have decided to go with UNC - Greensboro. While Radford, Wintrop, George Mason, UMBC, Marist, and a few others made good offers Ryan wants to play in the big time. Thanks for guiding us through this."
–Mike Galligan

Comments from Amazon Readers:

Reviewer: A reader from England
5 out of 5 stars. Just what I needed–information.
October 5, 2000

Everything you ever wanted to know about athletic recruiting when your high school coach doesn't do it for you. And here's a hot tip. You can go one better than your high school coach, Mom and Dad. Check out the opportunities at West Point. Almost everyone there is a scholar-athlete, and all on full scholarship plus getting paid [...] a year! And, best of all, if you get hurt, you don't lose your scholarship! In conclusion, Wayne Mazzoni did a great job. His, "Athletic Recruiting & Scholarship Guide" is the book that tells you everything you need to know.

Reviewer: A reader from Fairfield, NJ United States
5 out of 5 stars. Excellent advice; an easy read for high school athletes!
December 9, 1998

While this book does not have the perfect layout of pictures, etc. that many books do, it has the only thing you really need when it comes to recruiting...an insiders perspective on the process. This book can be read in a few hours and your learning curve during this time will be dramatic. I am so much more prepared now then when I started this process.

Reviewer: net-return from Charlotte, North Carolina
5 out of 5 stars. Excellent! All the information.
December 1, 1998

Our players found this book to be very helpful. The book's size was not intimidating yet it hit all the bases in detail. I highly recommend the "Athletic Recruiting & Scholarship Guide."

Reviewer: An Amazon.com Customer
5 out of 5 stars. The exact information we needed.
October 5, 2000

After hearing the author speak on a sports radio station as an expert on recruiting, I bought the book. The book is easy to read and has all the information on the topic of recruiting outlined in a step-by-step method. He makes a confusing process, very easy to follow. I recommend it highly.

Reviewer: A reader from Fairfield, NJ USA
5 out of 5 stars. Wayne's book is all that and more.
September 11, 1999
Though a little skeptical based on one person's review that the book was "lean" in terms of graphics, I went ahead and bought it. While I agree that the book is not gorgeously laid out, it has some of the best information I have ever read in a how to book. My learning curve went straight up and not only would I recommend this book to any parent but have also bought copies for friends.

Reviewer: A reader
5 out of 5 stars. Excellent.
June 23, 1999
I thought I did everything for my son that I could...When it came time for college, we just hit a brick wall. Wayne has helped us break through that wall. Step by step. Our family owes a great deal to Wayne. Thank you!

Reviewer: A reader
5 out of 5 stars. A great book.
June 23, 1999
This book made it clear what we need to do. I can't wait to get started on helping my daughter get a place to play in college and a scholarship.

Reviewer: A reader from Austin, Texas
5 out of 5 stars. A big, big help.
June 16, 1999
This book was exactly what I needed. I didn't realize how much I didn't know until I read this book. This should be required reading for every high school athlete and their parents.

Reviewer: A reader
5 out of 5 stars. Thank you so much.
June 16, 1999
As a high school football and baseball coach, I think it is one of my jobs to help kids move to the next level, but since I never recruited, I really did not know that much about the process. After reading this book, I feel I know almost all of it and I surely know more of what my roll should be.

Reviewer: A reader
5 out of 5 stars. It gets results.
June 14, 1999

Not sure if the author reads this, but this book taught me so much in a short period of time. The coach at the school really didn't know what to do, so we had nowhere to turn. This book gave us the entire process and was easy to understand. Thanks again.

Reviewer: A reader
5 out of 5 stars. I've read them all and this one is the best!
June 14, 1999

My son was just offered a $10,000 a year scholarship. Obviously he had the talent, but this book showed us how to get the coaches attention. I am convinced this offer would not have come through without reading this book.

Reviewer: A reader from Portland, Oregon
5 out of 5 stars. Thank you!
June 14, 1999

I work as a high school guidance counselor and was told to learn as much as possible about the recruiting process for sports. I bought all the books on the market and this one was BY FAR the best book out there. We bought copies for all our student-athletes.

Reviewer: A reader
5 out of 5 stars. Perfect. Just what was needed.
June 11, 1999

My son's high school coach gave him a copy of the book and he read it in two days. Now he is leading the effort to get himself a scholarship. The book is inspiring and effective for high school athletes.

Reviewer: An Amazon.com Customer
5 out of 5 stars. Excellent. A must have for students and parents.
March 13, 1999

I was curious to see what the book was about since I had seen Wayne speak and heard him on TV. Reading one of the reviews on this site, I was skeptical. Not any more. Unless you expect the book to magically turn into a scholarship offer, you will find that it is amazing. It tells you exactly what to do and how to do it. Really the perfect how to book.

Reviewer: A reader from Connecticut
5 out of 5 stars. The best college sports recruiting guide available.
December 31, 1998
Mr. Mazzoni explains the whole deal... not only offers great advice but shows students and parents HOW to get it done! Buy it!

Reviewer: A reader from Salt Lake City, Utah
5 out of 5 stars. Perfect.
December 2, 1998
Wayne Mazzoni has written, clearly and effectively, the best college sports recruiting guide available. It covers all the difficult and unknown questions for parents and student athletes, from how to choose a school, to how to promote yourself as an athlete to the schools of your choice. This book helped me and my son a great deal and is a must for anyone interested in playing collegiate sports.

Reviewer: An Amazon.com Customer
5 out of 5 stars. A must read for athletes and their parents.
December 2, 1998
This book is just what I was looking for. It was easy to read (which meant my son could read it too) and follow. The baffling recruiting process now seems so simple.

Reviewer: An Amazon.com Customer
The recruiting process is so confusing, that athletes and their parents (who are going through the process for the first time) need to learn the reality of recruiting. This book explains the problems with getting your child noticed and how to overcome them. Plus, it was written by a former college coach who knows first hand what recruiting is like.

The Athletic Recruiting & Scholarship Guide

For High School Athletes and Parents

ALL SPORTS GRADES 9-12

Learn the Secrets to Maximizing Exposure to
Coaches and Achieving Scholarship Potential

WAYNE MAZZONI
Mazz Marketing, Inc.

The Athletic Recruiting & Scholarship Guide
For High School Athletes and Parents

By Wayne Mazzoni

Published by: Mazz Marketing, Inc.
287 Cortland Avenue
Black Rock, CT 06605

FOREWORD

Coach Wayne Mazzoni has a motor that is always running in one direction; forward. I have never met an individual, in coaching or out, that has as much energy and enthusiasm that Coach Mazzoni does. We both had sports in the forefront of our lives when we first met and it is a very passionate part of who we are. Since we were both young, we had always longed to pursue a future in athletics, whether in the professional or collegiate ranks. Both of us knew that when we got older, we either would be playing, teaching or doing both in the great game of baseball.

Living nearby to Teikyo Post University, Coach and I crossed paths and developed a great friendship, a friendship bound together by our love of coaching. I first noticed in him the desire and willingness to work towards perfection and excellence with his team and in all the areas off the field to help his program. From Wayne I learned much fundraising and how he basically took a program that was on the bottom to a level the program has never seen. It was only through hard work and dedication that he was able to enhance the program the way he did. I don't think there is anybody (and I mean anybody) who could have done the things Wayne has done with his team. Coach Mazzoni is constantly in a fundraising mode in an effort to provide things for his team which they previously never had; trips to Hawaii and Florida, indoor practices at batting cages and indoor domes, buying equipment to better his team or giving gifts to his the seniors from whom he has demanded so much, coach Mazzoni does it all for the love of the game and the desire to improve others. His recruiting efforts have been amazing. The team he inherited in 2000 had only thirteen players. Going into the 2004 season he will have 30 players on varsity and fifteen on a newly created junior varsity program. The man knows about recruiting.

I believe in the righteous pursuit of excellence in anything we do and only through a strong work ethic and dedication can this be done. This common bond brought our friendship and mutual admiration to new levels. Having worked with him on the field, I have seen him in action and it is awesome. He coaches players up and instructs young men in the details of the game. I can honestly say that there are not many better, if any at all. Recruiting has always been a specialty area for Coach Mazzoni. It is no surprise to have found out that his energy and enthusiasm has made him an expert in this area of collegiate coaching. Wayne has continued to bring in better ball players to TPU annually.

This book provides a rare insight to the recruiting process and is done as well as any book of its kind. It is so good that the college placement director where I work and coach (The Salisbury School (CT)), uses this book to help kids at our school learn the college recruiting and choosing process. It is no wonder that over one hundred high schools in the New York, New Jersey, and Connecticut area have brought Wayne in to lead workshops on this topic.

Though I played major league baseball after being drafted out of high school, I was heavily recruited as a quarterback and was very close to attending Clemson University before the draft. I know first hand that this book is reality regardless of the sport that you play. I am confident that you too will find this book to be a gem, the best of its kind! My recommendation is that you keep it on the top of your bookshelf and read it over and over again. I know that you will benefit greatly from the teachings and helpful hints that you will find inside. Good luck in your journey in choosing the college that is right for you. Be bold, be courageous and most of all, maintain your integrity. Wayne Mazzoni has worked hard to bring you a fine book and if you bring the same passion to your goals, you will be as successful as he is.

- Rico Brogna, Former Major league Baseball player

CONTENTS

INTRODUCTION

You're a high school student-athlete (or parent). You have thought about playing sports in college. You have heard a little about the recruiting process from friends, teammates, coaches, and counselors, yet it all seems a little confusing. There are many things you have thought about. At which school will I be the happiest? Am I good enough to play college sports? What level of competition would be best for me? How can I get the attention of college coaches? Can I get into the schools I want? Am I good enough for a scholarship? What should I know about the athletic programs that recruit me? How do I make my final school decision?

These are all legitimate questions. This guide will help provide these and many other answers. For any student-athlete thinking of going to college and participating in sports, there is a specific process involved. This book will guide you through that process in nine distinct stages.

The first is deciding which schools make the best match for you. This is best done without considering athletics as a factor. For many reasons, you should first choose colleges you would like to attend on a non-athletic basis. Only after you have reached a target list of schools, should you then narrow down further using athletics as a factor. The first section of this book will give you the criteria to make an intelligent decision on which of the thousands of colleges would be most suitable for you.

The second step is to determine which of these colleges meet your athletic skills and goals. This section will explain the differences in college athletic divisions and give you a clear cut way to determine what school is best for your talent level. Further, I will cover the type of situation that is best for incoming freshman. Many athletes have gotten into the wrong athletic situation because of a lack of understanding of the recruiting process. This will give you the opportunity to learn from those before you who have made mistakes.

After narrowing down the list of target schools, step three will show you why it is hard to get coaches to notice you. Many times athletes think that because a coach did not contact them, they are not good enough to play at that school. I will explain why nothing could be farther from the truth. I will then cover the recruiting process from the coaches' point of view to show how difficult it is for them and how this affects you.

Step four teaches you how to overcome the problems of the recruiting process and take matters into your own hands. Simply put, this section will teach a specific set of methods you can use to get exposure to college coaches. It is impossible to say whether or not the coach will want you to play for their program, but at least you will be evaluated.

The next section discuses the various eligibility and recruiting rules one needs to meet in order to participate in college athletics. An overview of these rules and the function of the NCAA Clearinghouse will be covered.

In the sixth chapter, I will provide you with a list of questions to ask both players and coaches at schools you are considering. Most student-athletes fail to ask questions and find out upon arrival at the school that the real situation is completely different from the one they had imagined.

The next section will discuss how to maximize your chances of getting accepted into the schools you desire. If you have the perfect school and athletic situation, but don't get accepted, nothing else matters. No one can promise to get you into a school, but there are some clear-cut ways to maximize your chances. That will be the focus of the seventh chapter.

In the eighth section, you will learn how to maximize your scholarship potential. Once a coach has shown interest, there is a specific set of questions you can ask that will help you determine if any scholarship money is available to you. Many qualified athletes never get any athletic money because they don't ask for it. If you want more money on a job, ask for a raise. You may not get it, but it is better than waiting for someone to reward you when they are ready. By reading this section, you will learn all about the athletic scholarship process.

Finally, the last section will discuss how to make the final choice of schools. After narrowing down schools based on non-athletic and athletic factors, maximizing exposure to coaches, becoming eligible, giving yourself the best chance to be accepted, and maximizing your scholarship potential, you will be left with one more decision. Which one of the several schools you are considering do you choose? How do you come to this conclusion? This section will give you a guide to this process.

First, some facts about recruiting. As of 2002, there were:

NCAA Participation

- 84,592 NCAA Division I male athletes. 62,667 NCAA Division I female athletes.
- 45,184 NCAA Division II male athletes. 29,680 NCAA Division II female athletes.
- 78,705 NCAA Division III male athletes. 56,930 NCAA Division III female athletes.
- This totals – 210,984 NCAA male athletes. 150,916 NCAA female athletes.
- This totals – 361,900 total athletes in all levels of the NCAA.

High School Participation

- Based on the National Federation of High School Athletics, as of 2002 there were approximately 10,000,000 high school athletes.

The Result

- Simple math will tell you that 3% of high school athletes will go on to play in college.

Playing college sports is tough; it is a privilege and an honor. Above and beyond anything that I can tell or teach you in this book, is that the best way to get recruited is to be a good player. Being a standout player on your high school team and summer or travel team will get you recognized. In addition to being a good player, it is important that you are a good person. College coaches want to work with players who are coachable, respectful, and hard working. The majority of college coaches are not coaching Division I football and basketball, which means that they do not have the pressure of big salaries, national championships, boosters, etc. They coach because they like working with good kids, they like teaching, and they love their sport. Just about every coach I interviewed for this book said that they would not take a player who was talented, but a problem. In short, work hard on and off the field and be as a good a person as you can.

Only the dedicated athletes will go on to play their sport in college. Set up the proper work ethic for yourself as soon as you can.

College Life

It is now time to begin this process, but before you do keep your end goal in mind. College should be the best four years of your life. You will spend these years learning, making friends, becoming responsible, and having fun. If you are one of the lucky few who play college athletics, this should add to your experience. If you received a scholarship, congratulations, I am sure your parents are happy. But always remember, whatever happens to you in college and in life, never stop striving to be your best. The Japanese have a word for this; Kaizen. It means constant improvement in small increments. Keep working hard to achieve your goals and live life to the fullest. If you do so, more often than not you will have a wonderful life, full of great experiences and memories. I wish you luck!

CHAPTER ONE

NARROW YOUR LIST OF COLLEGES

A Major Life Decision

Choosing a college is one of life's major decisions. For most students, it is the biggest one they will make in their young lives. Much of the trouble in selecting the right school comes from a lack of information about the process. Students, most of whom have never been on a college campus, are asked to choose from the thousands of colleges across the nation. Often they receive information from many different sources; guidance counselors, teachers, former students, friends, parents, and siblings, which is often contradictory. Further, they do not have a set of guidelines to help them reach an intelligent decision.

While it would be convenient to say that all colleges are the same and that any choice is fine, it simply is not true. Choosing the wrong school, for any number of reasons, can lead to problems, some which can impact on the rest of one's life. Further, when factoring in the desire to compete in college athletics, the decision becomes increasingly difficult. Because schools have different goals academically and athletically, it takes a great amount of personal understanding and research to know that the situation one is entering is best suited for oneself.

This chapter is designed as a guideline to help students (and their parents) make intelligent decisions about colleges. At this point athletics will not be a factor in choosing which colleges are best for you. Should you decide not to play all four years; get hurt, get cut, the school drops the sports, etc., it makes sense to be at a school you like regardless of the sports.

On average only 25% of all athletes that enter college as freshman athletes will continue to play through to their senior year. This means that SEVENTY-FIVE percent will stop playing somewhere along the way. The reasons could be as follows; they got cut, hurt, decided it was no fun, decided that it took too much time, rather concentrate on studies, job search, work, friends, relationship, etc, etc. etc.

The fact is that if you pick a school simply because you like the athletic program but not the school, how do you think you will feel about that college if you are no longer playing? This is why I emphasize that you need to find a school that fit your desires first, then determine which match up athletically.

75% of high school athletes that enter college as freshmen athletes will not be playing by their senior year.

The following are factors that will help you narrow down your list of colleges.

Location

Consider the following when deciding how far away from home is acceptable:

- Do you want to drive to and from school? Or fly? Not only does the latter take more time, but it is also a cost that will add up over your four years.
- Do you plan to go home a lot? This is easier if you are closer to home.
- Will you have a car on campus?
- Can you drive home when you want or will you be stranded on campus or dependent on friends or mass transportation to travel home?

- Do you want friends and family to be able to visit you and see your athletic games once in a while or often? Some parents want to watch all of the children's games. Some children want their parents to see all their games. Some don't.
- Are you looking for a particular climate for enjoyment or sports reasons? In other words, don't go to Florida if you want to ski, and year-round golf is tough in Maine.
- Will you feel comfortable moving far away?

There are many things that distance away from home will affect while you are in college. For example, if you are far away from home, chances are you will spend certain holidays and breaks at school or with friends who live closer to campus, if you cannot afford the ticket home. To some this is fine, but to others it is unacceptable. If you are unsure of whether this factor will make a difference, think back to past events. Did you enjoy being away at summer camp or did you get homesick? Do you enjoy sleeping at friends' houses or would you rather be in your own bed and home? How have you felt on vacations or other trips away from home?

If you do not care whether you are 10 feet or 3,000 miles from home, this is fine. You can use the other criteria to narrow down your list. If distance to home is a factor, decide how far is acceptable and being with those schools.

Setting: Urban, Suburban, Rural

The second part of location is the setting of the school. That is whether the school is located in a city, suburb, or rural area. This has an impact on the type of college life you will have. Going to school in New York City is much different than going to school in Topeka, Kansas. Social life, dorms, parties, and athletics will most likely be different. The best way to decide on these factors is to visit campuses in the different settings or refer back to trips you made to such places. No one place is better than the other, just different.

In addition, keep in mind that some schools may be in a rural area, but only a short trip from a large city, while others have country surrounding them for hundreds of miles. This decision alone narrows down college selection immensely. For example, if you decide that you want to be within five hours driving distance from your home and in the suburbs, you have eliminated thousands of schools.

Number of Students

Many students have gone to colleges with as few as 300 people, others to schools that have classes with 300 people. There are small (100 - 3,000), medium (3,000 - 10,000), large (10,000 - 20,000), and huge (20,000 - 50,000+) schools from which to choose. Life at a small college usually consists of smaller student to teacher ratios, resulting in personal relationships, and close attention from professors and administrators.

Of course, it also means that everyone knows what you ate for breakfast and that you got a D on your last test. However, if you like being the big fish in the small pond, this may be the way to go.

Large schools, on the other hand, often offer big-time athletics, national reputations, published professors, many parties and social events, large classes, and often an abundance of money for items such as facilities and equipment. Interestingly however, many people at large schools find that they socialize only with a small number of people. Since it is impossible to know all the students, people can feel lost and stick with the group with which they feel comfortable.

Use the number of students to further narrow your list of target schools.

Cost

Unfortunately for most families, money is high on the list of decision-making factors. Depending on your family's financial situation, money may play a role in choosing a college. Some schools, especially in-state public schools, are much less expensive then private colleges, although tuition is rising at these institutions also. The average total cost for a year of public school education in 1996 was $9,285.

Many private schools now cost as much as $1,000 per week, which is more than the weekly income of about 70 percent of the country's households. The average cost of a private school is $17, 631.

Tuition is on the rise in general, as is room, books, board, and the amount needed for spending money. It is not uncommon these days for an education to cost $150,000. While there are possibilities of loans, financial aid, academic and, athletic scholarships (more about this later), let's assume, for the moment, none of this is available to you.

You and your family must decide what price range is acceptable. If any cost is feasible, consider yourself lucky and move on to the next topic. If not, your choice of schools will be narrowed down by price. I know of several people accepted at Ivy League schools, who were unable to afford them when aid packages did not come through. Therefore, it is wise to investigate the cost of schools.

As far as aid money is concerned, there are several factors that will help in this area. First and foremost is the theory that the early bird gets the worm. All funding sources are on a first-come first-serve basis to those who qualify. So get going with the forms! However, grants which are offered based on academic ability often are not given to people who apply early but to students who play hard to get and need money as an incentive to attend a certain school. Second, it helps to explore the many books which list scholarships for reasons you never would of thought possible. There may be money available to left-handed students with blonde hair, 3.4 GPA's, who are of Italian descent. Some are that off beat. But, if they are offering, why not partake?

Some ways you can get money for college are from Federally insured student loans. This is borrowed money that must be paid back after you graduate and only for needy students, which is determined by your families expected contribution. This contribution level is determined from a federal formula that considers income, assets, age, family size, and each earner's need for a retirement fund. The gap can be filled with loans, college grants, or a college job. Another way is Federally insured Parent Loans to Undergraduate Students (PLUS). This allows parents with good credit to borrow up to the full cost with a variable interest rate. College grants are tuition discounts offered to students that colleges particularly want. These are usually based on academic ability as opposed to financial need.

It is best to contact the financial aid director at the university to learn more about the program. But one piece of advice always holds true. First come, first serve.

There are also financial aid consultants that can help you with this process. They can be very helpful in gaining the best aid package available. They are often called education consultants and many are former high school counselors or college admissions workers. Check yellow pages for listings in your area.

Academic Reputation & Admissions Standards

The school's academics may influence your decision. Some students are not concerned with such items, but many are. In this regard, most students usually apply to schools that are below, equal, and above what they consider their academic ability to be. However, you must decide what you want from your college. Many students want to go to Harvard, but not everybody can, even if they have the grades.

It is my advice to attend the school with the best academic reputation at which you will be accepted, assuming the college meets your other criteria. The reason is simple: a college's reputation can help you as you pursue employment. Thus, the better the school the more influence it will carry with prospective employers. In addition, the difference in academic difficulty (how hard the classes are) between your most difficult college and second most difficult college will be minimal, if not non-existent.

If you have a particular calling or desire to major a certain field, find out if the school has such a department and inquire about its reputation. If you want to be a doctor, don't choose a school without a premed. major or you will be in for a shock upon arrival. Further, take into account the schools library and computer system. Are they sufficient and up to date? You need the resources to learn, make sure the school has them if you are concerned.

Social Life

This area is often overlooked by college-bound students. Social life is different at many schools. Some are based on the Greek system (fraternities and sororities), others are not. Some campuses have stringent alcohol and party restrictions, some don't. Some campuses have social events programmed into college life, while others don't. Some campuses are self sufficient to educate and entertain you, while others expect you to travel off-campus for fun.

In addition, many activities are centered around alcohol at schools, regardless of whether it is legal or not. If you do not approve of such behavior, I suggest choosing campuses where it plays less of a role. Again, there are many ways to learn what the schools social life is like. One way is to ask current or former students. Better yet, spend a few nights on campus, either on your own or hosted by a student to see first hand what a typical evening is like.

Campus Makeup

Like people, many campuses are different in their appearance. Much of this is due to geographical region and setting (urban, suburban, rural). Still, even two rural campuses could be totally different. Some schools are spread out, others cramped. Some have hills, others are flat. Some are new and modern, others old and historic. Some are filled with trees and lakes, others barren.

You must see as many campuses as you can to understand what you like and do not like about each school. You will be there at least four years (hopefully not much longer!) so you should enjoy the setting.

Some other factors to take into account. Are there:

- Intramural programs? This is a great source of fun for many students. Regardless of whether you play sports for all four college years or not, it is a good bet you will play intramurals. If you are like most people, you will have some of your fondest memories from intramural competition.
- Exercise rooms? Some campuses have wonderfully equipped state-of-the-art weight rooms. Other campuses don't have anything.
- Pools? If you are a recreational swimmer, and this matters, investigate before it is too late.
- Bowling alleys? Arcades? Pool tables? Fun, fun, fun. Does the campus have places for you to have fun?
- Student unions? A social place where people meet, learn about campus events, eat snacks, etc.
- Cafeterias that meet your standards? Most people complain about the food at colleges, find out if they have a point.
- Banks and ATM's on campus? For convenience purposes. If you spend too much money, maybe you don't want one on campus (or at least your parents don't!).
- Places to practice or play loud music? If you are a musician and want to practice, is there a place for you?
- Living options for freshmen, sophomore, juniors, and seniors? Will you be in a dorm for four years, a fraternity or off-campus?
- Places to study quietly? Library, study rooms in the dorms.

- Violence or problems on campus? Some schools have had troubles. While most of the time these are random, one-time incidents, it is wise to investigate the criminal history of the campus.

These and many others should be asked. If you have a particular concern, such as a handicap or health problem, then a whole other list of questions would be necessary. Again, this is your life for four years, take the time to research.

The Student Body
Factors to consider when looking at the student body of the school are the numbers and percentages of:

- Men? Women? Ratio of men to women?
- U.S. students? Students from each state?
- International students?
- Minority students?
- Students in the Greek system?
- Living on campus? Off campus? Commuters?
- Graduate students on campus?

If it is important for you know what type of people you will be going to school, socializing and making friends with, you should research the factors which matter to you.

Faculty
To many, the make up and reputation of the faculty is of great concern. Schools use a variety of instructors, with degrees ranging from B.A.'s to Ph.D.'s. If you believe that Ph.D.'s are best suited to teach, then you should choose a school where a high percentage of professors are Ph.D.'s. Do you want to learn from a professor who has just written his fifth book on nuclear physics or is that intimidating?

How To Get This Information
There are many ways to get the information that you will use to make intelligent decisions about your college choice. Information can be obtained from:

- The many books and magazines that list and rank various factors about the schools. Petersons publishes excellent college ranking guidebooks. US News and World Report and Newsweek Magazine rank colleges based on many factors in their yearly college editions.
- Calling the admissions departments and requesting information. It helps to have narrowed down your list somewhat before doing this or you will have a tired phone finger and the mailman will dislike you. Almost all colleges have Internet sites with the same information.
- Every college has a web site.
- Make a visit to the campus. Meet students, take a tour, sit in on classes, see a sporting event, etc. Try to live a day of a typical student.

Ask students the following questions:

- How would you rate the quality of the education?
- How has your experience been?
- What is the social life like?
- If you could do it all over would you pick this school? Why? Why not?
- What is the opinion of the athletes on campus?
- Speak with alumni. While most brag about their alma mater and only seem to remember the good things, they will give the honest scoop if they know you are counting on them for crucial information. Ask them the same questions listed above.

Again, as you are aware, all of the deciding factors above do not take athletics into account. Why not, you ask? Making choices based solely on athletic interests usually do not work in the long run. College is not just about playing sports. It is a comprehensive social and educational experience. Being in the wrong social or academic environment will make people unhappy, regardless of how well their sports career is going.

Further, while it is unfortunate, it is true that many people who go to college to play sports do not continue for all four years. Whether it is because they get injured, cut, or decide not to continue to play, it is ideal to be on a campus which you enjoy regardless of your sport. Ideally, the athletic and non-athletic aspects of your school both should suit you.

Stick Close to Home to Gather Info

Before venturing out all over the country to visit college you might be interested in, I suggest you take a weekend to ride around to the colleges within an hour or so of your home. Regardless of whether or not you would ever consider going to these schools, it will give you an idea of a variety of college campuses. By visiting schools small and large, in the city and country, it should give both you and your family a better idea of what you like. If you have a school near you that has 30,000 students and you love how big it is, then chances are these types of schools would be for you. If you feel overwhelmed, then go to a school with 3,000 students and love it, then you have gotten very valuable feedback. The more you know the better you will be at making a decision.

Goals

Your goals at this stage of the book/search process are to try identify your likes and dislikes. Once you are comfortable with what you are looking for, you can then come up with a list of anywhere from 5 to 50 colleges that generally meet your needs. Again, none of this takes into account your interest in athletics. That will come next.

QUICK SUMMARY:

- Since research shows that the majority of those who enter college to participate in sports stop playing somewhere along the way, it makes sense to begin your college search without factoring in athletics. There will be plenty of time for that later.
- The more you visit school, both near and far, the better you will be at knowing what you want out of college.
- The worksheet at the back of the book can help you with this step.
- Once you have a workable list of colleges that feel as if they might make a fit, you can proceed to the next step.

CHAPTER TWO

CHOOSING SCHOOLS BASED ON ATHLETICS

At this point you should have a target list of schools in mind. Now you must narrow this list down by athletic factors. First, you can eliminate the schools that don't have the athletic program you play. Quite simply, if you play soccer and five of the schools on your list don't offer soccer, scratch them off.

Next, you should separate the schools by the level of athletics.

The Various Levels

Florida State University and Williams College compete on different athletic levels. There are thousands of schools offering athletics, some at higher competition levels than others. This does not mean sports are more enjoyable for the participants at more competitive levels. Sports are sports; the focus is just different. In the NCAA (there is also NAIA, a lesser known governing body of college sports, and NJCAA for junior colleges) schools are broken down into Division I, II and III. Division I is the highest level and offers athletic scholarships (Division I football is broken into IA and IAA. The difference between A and AA is the number of scholarships offered (85 to 63) and the competition level. AA being below A).

Division II offers scholarships, but is considered a step below Division I competition.

Finally, Division III cannot offer any money relating to the athletic ability of the student-athlete and is generally a lower competition level than Divisions I and II.

Differences in levels are usually based on size, strength, and speed, as well as ability. In most cases, the higher the level the more media coverage, better facilities and accommodations for athletes and teams. Occasionally, some Division III teams are better than their Division I counterparts. This is rare and usually occurs in the non-revenue sports. The differences are generalized on the chart.

DIFFERENCES IN ATHLETIC DIVISIONS

	Division I	Division II	Division III
Athletics	Most Competive	Highly Competitive	Competitive (Ranges depending on team and sport)
Scholarships	Full or Partial (Some conferences do not offer scholarships, i.e., Ivy)	Full or Partial	None
Financial Aid	Based on need, academics, other talents. Grants, loans, and work study.	Based on need, academics, other talents. Grants, loans, and work study.	Based on need, academics, other talents. Grants, loans, and work study.
Time Commitment	Year Round	Year Round	Partial Year (Depends on school and sport.)

These groupings are general. Differences between Division I, II, and III vary greatly within an institution and individual sports programs. There are certain Division III programs that would be as good as or better then other Division I programs. Knowing how good a program actually is, is not easy to figure out. The best advice is to ask those in the know. Coaches, scout, trainers, etc. Further, you can check the schools website to see their record, opponents, awards of players, etc. For example, if you know team X is very good in softball, but know nothing about team Y. It might tell you quite a bit if you visit the website of either school and find out that Y beat X 15 - 2. Teams can change quickly at the college level so what held true for the past might not be that way now. Again, it is difficult to know until you investigate.

I am often asked what determines what schools are Division I, II or III. For the most part it is related to the schools philosophy of the role that athletics will play within the education. Division III athletics, based on their rules for limited practice and games and the fact that they don't offer athletic scholarships, makes them by nature less demanding then Division I. It certainly does not mean that the coaches as these levels don't want to win or don't take their profession seriously. You can bet they do. In fact, even at the Division III level many sports are becoming year round, even as the NCAA tries to legislate against it. For example, football may not be able to practice in the spring in Division III, but the culture at a particular school may be that all the football players get together to workout and the captains lead practices. Generally Division III schools have strong academic reputations and thus feel that sports is only a part of the whole educational process. In fact, at times when higher academic Division III schools win at a high level, there can become between winning and the schools philosophy. Typically winning requires tweaking the recruiting/admissions goals of the school, as well as showing that the students are taking a lot of their time working on their sport.

Division I athletics, especially for programs where many athletes are on scholarship can almost become a full-time job. To be a Division I athletic program, the schools basketball and football programs must have certain facility seating sizes. Often people thing that Division I schools are such because they have huge enrollment. But this is not the case. Certainly there are many large state universities that have Division I athletics, but there are also many Davidson's, Duke's, and Rice's out there that have smaller enrollment.

At Division I schools, academics can, but does not always take a back seat to athletics. There are many premier academic institutions in this country that treat student-athletes just as they would any student. Some schools, however, often give breaks to those athletes that spend almost all of their waking hours practicing, training, or playing their sport. Especially when you factor in the travel that is required of certain sports at certain schools.

Division II, being in the middle, is really just that. While they do offer athletic scholarships it is hard to make a generalization. Some schools have large facilities and a big emphasis on their programs; others do not. The majority of Division II schools are not on the highly competitive academic side. This does not mean to say that academics are taking lightly once the student is in the school, is simply means that those with very high grades and test scores out of high school, typically look at Division I or III schools.

How To Determine What Level Is For You

Once you know which of your target schools compete at which level, you must determine which level is best for you. It is human nature to want to compete at the highest level, but this is not possible for everyone. Choosing a school based on a realistic assessment of one's ability is crucial.

To determine what level is best for you, consider the following factors:

- Ask your high school and summer coaches what they think of your ability as it relates to college divisions. Be wary of answers. Some of these coaches have a good idea of where you fit in; others do not.

- Ask college coaches who have seen you play.
- Talk with former players from your school who have gone on to play college athletics.
- Enroll in summer camps where you can evaluate yourself against others.
- Go to athletic contests at various levels and see how you compare.
- Determine where you rank with others on your team and in your area. If you have received any awards this would be an indication that you are in the top percentage of players in your area.

Division I basketball and football are on TV all the time. How about a division III field hockey game? Seen one of those on ABC lately? The fact is that the best way to determine how you compare to the college level is to watch the team practice or play.

If you participate in individual sports such as swimming, golf, track and field, etc., it may be easier to determine what your level. If you are a golfer and you consistently shoot 98 and Division I athletes are shooting 77, it may be fair to say you should consider a lower level, unless you see significant improvement in the future.

From an athletic standpoint, most student-athletes will have a better chance to play and star at less competitive schools. However, if you are skilled enough to make it in big-time athletics, you have a good chance to play professionally and may well find employment due to your athletic popularity.

Coaches:
- What level does your high school coach feel you can play?
- How about summer/travel coach?
- Private instructor?
- College coaches that have seen you?

Players:
- How do you rate on your team?
- Your high school league?
- Summer team?
- Do you know any players that played with you that now play in college? What do they think of your level?

Camps:

- If you attended a college camp, did they rate you?
- How did you feel you ranked with the group of players at the camp?
- Are you aware of any showcase camps in your area?

Skills:

- How do you compare physically?
- Are you fast, strong, quick?
- Do you have poor, average, outstanding skills?
- How much potential do you still have?

Visits:

- When visiting the college, see if you can get a chance to watch the team practice or play.
- There is no better feedback on how you compare then watching the team at the next level.

Possible Athletic Situations

What comes to mind is the movie Rudy. Rudy was determined to play football for Notre Dame. He did not have the size or skill of the others, but through his motivation he was on the team for four years and wound up playing in the last play of the last game of his career. While most everyone was inspired by this movie, as a recruiting advisor I would rather have seen Rudy go to a less competitive football school and play most of his career. It is not that I don't think dreams are great, but if playing is the goal, you must be realistic. Again, everyone is different. There are several ways a college athletic career can turn out. Here are the possible scenarios:

In the worst-case scenario, you attend a school that is way above your athletic ability and you don't make the team. Or, you make the team, but realize you will never play. At this point you either retire to intramural sports (fun, by the way!) or transfer. Many have done both. If you choose to stay on the team for four years even though you will not play, that is fine, if you are happy with the situation.

In another scenario, you are immediately the best player on the team, and while you have a dream career, a certain part of you knows you should have played at a higher level. This is better than the first case, but not the best situation. Of course, if you are at the highest level and start right away, good for you.

The ultimate situation, in my opinion only, is when you don't play at all or play sparingly your first year. Your second year, you play a good amount of the time, but are not yet a starter. Third year, you start and contribute to your team's success, but are not the leader. Senior year, you are a true team leader, and have your best season. As it is with any goal, it is best if worked for. Many student-athletes have had versions of these three cases.

Circle the levels that you feel are right for you:

Low Division III	Mid-Level Division III	High Level Division III
Low Division II	Mid-Level Division II	High Level Division II
Low Division I	Mid-Level Division I	High Level Division I

Narrow Again

Once you have a good idea of what level(s) is right for you, you can go back to the original list of schools you had from the last chapter. From that list your should be able to find five to eight schools that have athletic programs at the level you feel is best for you. This becomes your target list of college. You can then begin to get exposure to these college coaches.

The advantage of choosing which schools you would like first is that you know where you will be happy and why. I have seen many people choose a school based solely on the fact that a coach from that school recruited them. They did not know anything about the school or what their preferences for college were, they just went because someone showed interest. More often than not, this leads to an unhappy situation.

Since you have given the time and effort to make an intelligent decision, it is more likely you will be happy in the long run. Now, if you are already being recruited (calls, not letters) by coaches at your target schools, great. You are ahead of the game. If not, the next chapter will help you get exposure to these coaches. Further, if you are being recruited by a few coaches on your list, it doesn't mean the others don't want you, they just don't know about you. It is time for that to change.

Go to the appendix to see what schools are listed in your sport at the various levels. Visit www.mazzmarketing.com for resources to help you get more information about the schools and athletic programs you are interested in.

CHAPTER THREE

THE CONFUSING RECRUITING PROCESS

If you made the All-American team, skip this chapter.

If you are one of the best athletes in your state or have been recruited by college coaches since 9th grade (the year you become eligible to be contacted by coaches) then you can happily skip this section and move onto the next chapter.

Unfortunately, the rest of us either get either limited or no interest from college coaches. Does this mean we should pack it in and give up? Should we assume that because coaches didn't come knocking on our door that we don't have what it takes to play at the next level? NO, NO, NO, NO, NO, NO, NO, NO, NO, NO, NO, NO, NO, NO, NO, NO! What it does mean is that the recruiting process is so confusing it can boggle the mind! Compared to college recruiting, finding a needle in a haystack is a piece of cake.

Recruiting Is Like A Job Search

While most students don't yet know what a job search is like, parents do. Imagine what the world of work would be like if people without a job just sat at home and waited for companies to call and offer them a job. No one would work! That is why we have this process called a job search where we send out resumes, network, read help wanted ads, and interview. While some companies will go to college campuses to recruit recent graduates, typically they go to the best schools and look for the best students. The rest of us must conduct a job search. We are the ones who are proactive. We seek companies and try to sell them our total package of skills, education, and personality. If they like us, then we bargain over what it will cost them to retain our services. If we come to an agreement, we go to work for that employer.

RECRUITING IS NO DIFFERENT! Student-athletes must be proactive and recruit the coaches and schools. Unless you are an unbelievably skilled player (similar to a Harvard graduate seeking work) you will have to show initiative in contacting coaches. Due to the fact that many college coaches do not have the time, staff, or budget to recruit as they would like, most settle into certain habits. They look at schools they know well or that are near to their college. Or, they have a network of certain high school coaches they use to help them recruit players. However, this still leaves many players undiscovered. Thus, high school student-athletes and their parents must be the initiators in the recruiting process. That is the essence of this Guidebook.

The Dating Game

Unfortunately dating works the same way. It would be nice if we could just sit home and have the person of our dreams fall into our lap, but it doesn't work that way. We must talk with people, share common interests, go on dates, etc. to find a mate. Now if you are one of the best looking people in the world and have a great personality (the equivalent of being an All-State player in sports) then people will probably want to get to know you. The rest of us must get out and start looking.

Again, recruiting works the same way. You cannot leave the process up to the college coaches. If you are a great player, then skip to the chapter, "How to Maximize Scholarship Money," because coaches will be beating down your door, and you only need to learn how to negotiate the best scholarship offer. If you are the top student at Harvard looking for a job, companies will find you. Just learn how to negotiate a salary. The other 99% of us have to do it the old fashion way. We earn it. You can earn a place on a college team and maybe even a piece of the 100,000 scholarships offered each year.

Why The Recruiting Process Is So Confusing

From the college coaches' point of view, many factors make recruiting difficult. First, there are millions of high school athletes, but only thousands of college coaches, creating a numbers problem.

A second problem is geography. Simply, coaches don't often hear about athletes who are at distant schools.

Third, most athletic programs have neither the budget, nor the coaching staff, which would allow them to travel and see all the players. Thus, unless an athlete is one of the top in the school or region, they will often be overlooked.

Fourth, high school coaches usually are of little help because there is no benefit for them to do so. Some high school coaches do everything they can to help get their players to the next level. Others could care less. If you have a coach who helps you, great. If not, this is not a problem. If you consider their point of view it is understandable why they are not more active. Many have other responsibilities such as classes, coaching, family, and don't have the sufficient amount of time to help you participate at the next level.

If you do have a coach who is very active in helping you, do all you can to show your appreciation. First of all, this is an extraordinary person. Secondly, this coach probably has aspirations of moving up to the college level and could help you again in the future.

So often I hear, "My coach screwed me. He didn't give me any help at all." Most don't. Deal with it. Just about all coaches want to see you do well and very few would intentionally try to hurt your chances of playing in college. In fact, most want you to do well. It only improves their reputation as a coach who produces good players. It is just that many do not have the time or the expertise.

A final word: Regardless of your relationship with your high school coaches, always show respect and have a good attitude towards them. This is for two reasons. First of all, most coaches selected their career to help kids like yourself be all that you can. This is a special calling and teachers and coaches should be respected for their commitment to you. Secondly, if you have a problem with a coach, not a minor issue, but a major problem, such as a bad attitude, vulgar mouth, wise guy, etc., the coach can have the power to hurt your chances of playing and receiving scholarship offers. All coaches want to work with players who are fun to coach and willing to learn. No one wants to take on a problem player. And, who knows more about your attitude then your high school coach. While most college coaches don't rely on high school coaches for their athletic evaluation (many do though), they will all ask about your character and attitude. So make the best impression you can. If you don't like your coach, you are then learning one of life's greatest lessons–making the best of a bad situation.

Fifth, guidance counselors would often like to help you, but they usually have too much work to take the time to work with any one person in great detail. Further, their expertise typically is in college admissions, as opposed to college athletic recruiting. Again, these are great people, but should not be relied on to make or break your college recruiting process.

Sixth, you may not be getting adequate playing time. For example, you are a goalie on your high school soccer team. You are one of the best goalies in the region. Except the best goalie in the region is on your team. How do you get noticed? Are you still good enough to play at one of the hundred programs that offer soccer? You bet. But, unless you follow my system, how is a college coach to know how good you are?

Finally, less competitive teams often do the least recruiting. The Florida State football coaches will cover the country and contact who they need to contact. Smaller schools often don't. Therefore, if you are an average player, most likely no coaches will contact you, even though they would love to have you on their team. However, if you are not a superb athlete, but still want to play college sports, there is most likely a school out there that you will match with perfectly. Yet, most often an athlete will assume they were not good enough to play college athletics because coaches did not come beating down their door. Nothing could be farther from the truth. Unless an athlete is very poor, there is someplace to play, assuming they want to continue in college. So if you want to play college athletics, but college coaches aren't beating down the door, what do you do? You read on, of course!

You Become The Recruiter

If you want to work in the computer industry, do you expect IBM, Apple, and Microsoft to know about you and come looking to hire you? No. You write them or contact them. Whether they want you or not is their decision. Possibly they may want you, but as you learn more about the inner workings of the company you decide you would be happier someplace else. But you never know until you make the first move. If you went to the nation's top computer school (i.e. you are the best running back in the state) chances are one of those companies will track you down. If not, you do a job search. You target companies that may be in need of your skills, whether it be a smaller company, a start up, etc.

The same goes for the dating process. If you are at a party and there are five people of the opposite sex and one hundred of your sex, do you expect to get noticed? If you are gorgeous (i.e. throw a baseball 90 MPH) someone will probably talk to you. If you are average, like most of us, then the only way you can differentiate yourself from the others is by getting the courage to talk to the opposite sex.

Thus, the solution to this whole recruiting dilemma is to be proactive and recruit the coaches and schools you are interested in. This should be fairly easy if you have completed the first two chapters and have a workable number of schools targeted. Simply put, you do the recruiting. In business this is called marketing. The process by which companies make themselves and their products and services known to those who need them. I repeat, do not wait to be recruited, it may never happen. If it does, you are in the top percentile of athletes who ever hear from a college coach.

Further, do not confuse getting a letter from a college coach with being recruited. Many schools mass mail letters to student-athletes. Most likely the coach has never heard of you, but you still received a letter anyway. If you receive a phone call you are being recruited. If you send in materials and a coach writes back this is different. This is a form of communication whereby the coach knows who you are. Initial contact letters are often mass mailed. Don't be fooled into thinking you do not have to actively market yourself.

The recruiting process is confusing. It is inexact. If you sit and wait to get found, you will not unless you are a premier talent. This means you must be proactive.

Where Coaches Get Names of Prospects

Coaches get names of players from several sources; high school coaches, subscription services, recruiting services, newspapers and other publications, other college coaches.

Many college coaches have relationships with high school coaches and trust them enough to take referrals about players. Unfortunately many college coaches don't trust high school coaches for several reasons. First, they believe, whether accurately or not, that high school coaches aren't as qualified to judge talent as they are. Secondly, they may not believe the coach knows very much about the sports he or she is coaching. Third, they may have been burned before. If a high school coach speaks very highly of a player and that coach recruits the athlete only to find out that they were not nearly as good as advertised the high school coach's creditability is hurt. Thus, sometimes high school coaches can help, other times they cannot, and sometimes they hurt.

Subscription services are sometimes used by college coaches to get lists of prospects' names. These services are compiled by various scouts and are sold to college coaches.

Many recruiting services have sprouted lately which can provide you with a resume and other related services. But beware, many of these places can be helpful, yet they are after in business to make money and some will tell the coach anything just to make you sound better. This is a problem for many reasons.

First, you want to go to a program where you legitimately fit in, not one that is way above your abilities. Second, if coaches receive exaggerated praising and make the effort to come see you, and you are not nearly as good as expected, you are finished in their eyes and he may even hurt your chances elsewhere.

Third, because these services exaggerate so often, a coach may not believe a word he hears about you, even if it is true. Fourth, some of these businesses represent so many athletes that it is impossible for them to actually know who you are and what your skills are, and what you are looking for. So choose wisely for your recommendations. Finally, coaches are looking for self-starters, people with inner motivation. If you can do all this work yourself, you are showing them how much you care. How would it look if you sent someone to look for your job or meet someone of the opposite sex for you? There are employment agencies and dating services, but it usually works out better when you do it on your own. Besides with the information I provide you, you can do a better job and make more appropriate choices than a recruiting service can.

Another way college coaches compile names of prospects is through newspapers and magazines. Many papers will write stories about talented player or give statistical information. Many will list award-winning players. Some sport specific magazines will provide lists of top prospects that coaches can use.

Coaches typically compete for athletes. So one would wonder how many coaches get names of prospects from other coaches. Usually it is when they discover that an athlete is either too skilled or too unskilled to compete at his/her level. In this case they would pass the name on to another school to be helpful and possibly get names in return. For this reason it makes sense to conduct yourself in a professional manner regardless who is recruiting you.

Now if coaches have used these methods and are contacting you already, great! You are ahead of the game, but keep in mind the following. Just because certain coaches are recruiting you, it doesn't mean the ones who are not aren't interested. Chances are they don't know about you. If you are a football player who has always wanted to attend Stanford University in California, but only Rutgers, Syracuse, and Boston College are recruiting you, it doesn't mean Stanford doesn't want you. They may not know who you are.

Thus, if you are being recruited, but not by the schools that you want or you aren't being recruited at all, it is time to learn how to market yourself. Congratulations, you are now a recruiter. You are recruiting college coaches. Here goes...

CHAPTER FOUR

MAXIMIZE EXPOSURE
TO COLLEGE COACHES

How You Recruit The Coach
There are many ways to do this, but it must be done right. The following methods should be used:

The Letter
Write an introductory letter to the coach stating why you are interested in attending that school and playing for that coach. This will set you apart from 90% of the other athletes. Most likely you will receive a letter and questionnaire in return. The coaches may even contact you, depending on their interest.

The fact is that in this day of information it is very easy to learn more about the school, coach, and athletic program. Writing a letter, which shows you have done your homework will set you are from the others who simply write one generic letter and send it to coaches.

Sample Letter from Student-Athlete to Coach

September 10, 2003

Mr. John Doe
Head Sport Coach
University of Scholarship Offers
Athletic Field House
College Town, USA 12345

Dear Coach Doe:

I am a senior at Northport High School and I am interested in attending the University of Scholarship Offers next fall. During my high school career, I have been a member of the varsity football and baseball teams, but want to play only baseball in college.

Please review my enclosed athletic profile sheet. I think it provides an accurate description of my baseball and athletic ability. You can contact Mr. Bill Coach at Northport High School or Mr. Fred Scout for specific details regarding my playing abilities and attitude. I will also enclose a copy of my schedule should you have the time to attend a game.

I would appreciate any information you could send me about your program. I believe I know a good deal about it, but more information would help. Please include financial aid information.

I look forward to hearing from you and to having the opportunity to play for you in the near future.

Yours in Baseball,
Wayne Mazzoni

> *This is a very simple letter simply showing the coach that you took the time to find a bit about the school and the athletic program.*

The Resume

In order to be one step ahead of the questionnaire, you can enclose an athletic resume with your letter. It should list the following information:

Basic information:
Name, address, phone number
School name address, phone number

List academic information:
- GPA and class rank
- PSAT, SAT, ACT scores
- Intended major and career goals
- Extra-circular activities
- Any academic awards (Honor society, etc.)

Next, you list your athletic information:
- Height
- Weight
- Primary position and hand (L/R).
- League
- Pertinent sports statistics
- Awards/Honors, if any (Captain, All-League)
- Other sports you play

List your physical characteristics, such as:
- Speed, Strength
- Factors relevant to your sport (i.e., vertical leap for basketball, MPH for pitchers, bench press for football, number of goals in soccer, 40 time for most sports, etc.)

Sample Athletic Resume

Wayne Mazzoni
12 Not Telling Road
Sometown, NY 11768
(516) 555-1234

Northport High School
Laurel Hill Road
Northport, NY 11768
(516) 261-9000

Academic Data:

High School Average: 90.3 Class Rank: 78 of 523
SAT: 550 V, 680 M. Taking again: 12/2003
Planned course of study: Marketing
Career Goals: Sports Marketing

Athletic Data:

Height: 5'10 Weight: 175 lbs.
Position: Pitcher (Throw Left, Bat Left)
League: Suffolk County League II
Baseball:

Year	W-L	IP	ERA	H	K	BB
2001-02	6-1	75.3	1.75	50	85	12
2000-01	3-3	44	3.21	39	44	15
1999-01	1-4	29	4.43	29	24	18

Related Facts: Fastball clocked By Fred Scout (Brewers) at 84 MPH

Awards:

1997-8 All-county Pitcher. 2nd in Wins and ERA
1996-7 1st Team All-League Pitcher. K'd 15 one game.
1995-6 Only Freshman on Varsity

Other Sports Data: Football: Team Captain 1997-8. All-League.

References:

Mr. Bob Coach
Varsity Baseball Coach
Northport High School
(516) 261-9000 ext. 333

Mr. Fred Scout
Scout
Milwaukee Brewers
(516) 555-4321

*Again, this resume alone will not get you recruited. It will
simply give the coach some facts on which they can decide
if they want to read more or learn more about you.*

Game Schedules

Coaches will keep your schedule on file and go see you if they are very interested or happen to have the time to see you. Remember, however, that your season is their season and they have more game days, so it may be difficult to see you during the season. Don't just put your high school game schedule, put your travel team or summer league team or any other team on which you play. You never know when the coach might be able to see you play. If you will be at any tournament or showcase camps, let them know.

Photo

If you have an up to date photo, it would help to send it along. First, it helps the coach to see your physical appearance. Secondly, when they come to see you they already know who you are.

Press Clips

Most of the time press clippings from the newspaper are an instant source of verification of your ability. It is a third party who is unbiased making a positive statement about your ability. Coaches are sometimes wary of trusting press clippings because they may not be aware of the writer or league you play in. If you are a softball player who hit .750 for the season, many coaches will think you played in a weak league and thus have inflated statistics. That is, unless they are already familiar with your level of competition.

References

What can further separate you from the crowd are your references. If you can list any people, such as a coach, scout, alumni, etc., who can attest to your athletic abilities and personal characteristics, this will help you get recruited by coaches. If you do not have anyone like this available to you, it would help to seek them out. Remember, when a coach receives your letter and resume, the first thing he will do is try to verify your information

Sample Letter of Recommendation

Dear Coach:

I would like to take this opportunity to recommend Wayne Mazzoni for your baseball program. I have known Wayne since 1994 when I first coached him on the Long Island Tiger Junior Baseball Team. I have coached him the past three years, including private lessons. I am now a scout for the Milwaukee Brewers.

Wayne would fit in well with any college program for several reasons. First, his baseball skills are superior to most players his age. He is a student of baseball, very coachable and thirsty for knowledge. He is a leader on and off the field by example and word. He was elected captain of both his varsity baseball and football teams at Northport High School.

From a baseball stand point, Wayne is ready to contribute at the college level. His pitching mechanics are solid, although he has a tendency to rush his delivery. He consistently throws strikes. Based on my radar clockings, he's in the low 80's and will only throw harder as he continues to grow.

He has an above average breaking ball that is tough against lefties. However, his best pitch is a change up. He baffles right-handed hitters with the pitch, especially at this age when most people cannot throw the pitch with such touch. He is somewhat of a Tom Glavine style pitcher, same pitching style and savvy. His pickoff move is exceptional and he fields his position with pride. He is a leader on the mound. Most professional teams are aware of Wayne; however, until he develops the ability to throw harder, it's difficult to convince anyone to draft him. This makes him ideal for college, however.

In addition, to his baseball skills and leadership, Wayne brings a great attitude and personality to any team. He is a fun player to coach. He is mature enough to have an intelligent conversation, yet young enough to be a leader of team antics if the time is right. Being so consistent on the mound, he knows occasional goofing off won't hurt his production. Of course, on game day he is a trained killer. No jokes, all business.

It is without reservation that I recommend Wayne Mazzoni for your baseball program. I can be reached at 516.555.4444, if you have any additional questions.

Yours in Baseball,
Fred Scout
Milwaukee Brewers

Video

Now, all the work you have done with the letter, resume, schedule, paper clippings, and references are designed to do one thing: get the coach to see you in action. But, there is one major stickler to this process. Your season is their season. If you are playing football every Saturday, so are they. You have a practice, so do they. So it is difficult to get the proper look. The way to overcome this challenge is to make a video.

Videos will set you apart from the crowd and will almost always be looked at by a coach. It is simply the best way to show your skills. Sports is a talent and the best way to show it is not on paper. If someone is a good drummer, do you think they can adequately display their drumming on paper? They could get some interest by describing their training, performances, etc. But, the best way would be to have someone hear them play live. If this is not possible, a video is the next best thing.

Video should consist of the following:

The opening should be a head shot of you. During this time speak about your qualifications. Basically this is a reading of your resume. This is necessary for several reasons. The coach may never look at your resume and this is a chance to tell them the information. If they have read it, repetition is the mother of learning, so it can't hurt to repeat it. Finally, coaches like to hear you speak. Are you confident, well spoken, serious or humorous? The best advice is to be yourself. This should be about 1 minute of film time.

It might sound like this:

"Hi coach, my name is Wayne Mazzoni, I am a junior at Northport High School on Long Island, New York. I am a 5'10, 175 pound running back, who runs a 4.7 40. I gained 650 yards last season and was selected captain for the upcoming year. I have a 3.5 GPA and am ranked 100 out of 425 in my class. I scored 1010 on my SATS, but will be taking them again in November and I will score higher. This summer I will be attending the Stonybrook Football Camp. Here is my highlight video. I am number 22. I hope to hear from you and good luck in your season."

- The next part of the video should be an individual showcase workout. Sport specific drills should be filmed from various angles. If you are a volleyball player, show serves, slams, bumps, sets, and other drills from as many different viewpoints. A football receiver would run patters, catch passes, etc. This should take about 3-5 minutes of film time.
- Next, game type action done in a practice situation. For example, if you are a quarterback show yourself dropping back and throwing to receivers in all different patterns. If you are a baseball player, show batting practice swings, ground balls from fungoe bats, or pitches to a catcher.
- If possible, and this takes work, most likely on your parents' part, include game film. If your school tapes games, use those. This can be one full game or a mixture of games that show you in the best light possible.
- Some sports do not bode well for a skills session. In that case, it should just be game or event tape.
- Finally, it is good to put a section of highlight tape at the end. Show all your best plays over time. Of course, for some this type of tape is impossible to get. But, remember any video is better than none

From years of experience watching these tapes I will tell you that there are several things you should do to make sure your tape gets the best possible opportunity to be seen.

First, do not use a full VCR tape with two hours of recording space available. If this happens, the coach may take your tape home and record "Seinfeld" reruns over it. Tapes should be about ten minutes in length and only the tape necessary should be on the reel. This may require professional services, but it pays in the long run.

Secondly, don't send tapes that you need to have returned. Make enough copies to go around. If a coach has to return your tape then 1) you are already a pain in the butt, 2) you will lose time while waiting for the return and 3) it could be damaged or lost on the way.

To further sell the importance of video, let me give you an example from my coaching days. A package came in the mail from a high school student athlete. He addressed the letter to me personally, not just

Dear Coach. He knew about my conference, my teams record, the team nickname, etc. In short, he wrote a great letter. That will get me to look further, right off the bat. I read his resume. It is well done and he has great academic and athletic numbers.

Now, I have the typical coach reaction. I am excited, but skeptical. He presents himself well, but if he can't pitch it doesn't do me any good. I read a few of his newspaper clippings. The kid sounds like the next Roger Clemens in the article, but for this particular person (he was from Canada) I don't know anything about his team or his league. He may be great, but I don't know the competition.

Next, I read a letter from a scout that I happen know. The scout loves him. He could be a draft prospect, but he wants an education. Now I'm excited. I'd love to go see him, but he plays in Canada. That would cost too much. Hold on...ah ha! He has a video. I put in the video. He makes his speech. It is obvious he is mature, both physically and mentally. Next he is pitching to a catcher on a practice mound. He throws well, good curve, good fastball, nice location. I see a few problems in his mechanics. I make a note and already want to work with him. I can make him better.

Next, he throws with a batter at the plate who is not swinging, but this shows me he can throw with a batter at the plate. Next, he pitches from the stretch, does a few pick off throws, and fields balls and bunts to the mound. Next, he shows his wind-up from different angles. The kid is legitimate.

Finally, he has two innings from a game he dominates. Now I realize he selected these two innings because he did well, but still I am sold. My next thought is who else go this package. I hope no one. I call the scout and he tells me the kid is not only a good pitcher, but has a great attitude. He loves to work hard.

I make a call, bring him in for a visit. He stays the weekend with guys on the team and they love him. I offer him a scholarship, and he picks another school. Darn!

But, that is a great example of how it should be done. Now if it turns out they he didn't show the Division I skills I was seeking, I would call him and tell him so and possibly offer to send his tape to a program and coach I think would be suitable for him. These packages work. It's time to get going on one!

One final point concerning the impact of video, consider the story of Wayne Chrebet, the New York Jets underdog wide receiver. Wayne attended Hofstra University and had an outstanding career. However, since no professional teams scout these games, he was an unknown. To prove his ability his father created a highlight tape and sent it to all of the teams in the NFL. Only one called. The Jets gave him a tryout where he excelled and he eventually made the team. After his first two years in the NFL he broke the record for the most receptions by a player in his first seasons. He continues to be a top-level receiver today. He is obviously talented, but the video tape gave him a shot. It could do the same for you.

> *The purpose of the video is so that the coach can see you playing. Ideally this would happen in person, but if not this is the next best thing. This may also entice the coach to make the effort to come see you play.*

> *Coaches want good players, not good video production qualities! Mom and dad's video camera is just fine.*

Camps

Another way to get exposure and be recruited by college coaches is to attend camps on college campuses. Camps take place all year around and offer exposure and the chance to learn from quality coaches. Often, summer camps are staffed by coaches from various colleges looking to find players. Thus, this is the time to make contacts and show what you've got. In addition, this also gives you the chance to spend time on a college campus to get a feel of what it is like. Check www.mazzmarketing.com for camp information.

Showcases

A recent development is the showcase camp. Often this takes place over two days and is simply an opportunity for coaches to see many players at once. For coaches who do not have large travel budgets, they attend showcase camps where many players can be seen. You have the opportunity to be seen in an individual workout and game situations. You can get lost in the shuffle sometimes, but have a good camp and the letters will come and the phone will ring off the hook. Before you sign up for any showcase you can ask either other athletes or parents who have attended. Further, you could call up a college coaches to see what their opinion is of particular showcases. Better yet, find out which ones they attend and sign up for those.

Updates
It is always good to update the information you sent to a coach. First, you name will stay fresh in his or her head. Second, coaches are impressed by the fact that you are keeping after them. You didn't just send them information and do nothing. You are persistent. Finally, it shows your sport progress. If you are a golfer and you sent information on your handicap, number of fairways and greens hit, average puts per round, etc., and all of these stats improve since you last sent your information, obviously you want them to know. I wouldn't send a resume to an employer stating that I only have an undergraduate degree when I have just received my Master's.

Information
There are many resources to find information about the coaching staff, team, schedule, field or court or rink, the number of players at each position. Each sport has a book and can be found by searching on my website. www.mazzmarketing.com. There are not books I have written, rather resources that are published by others that I have found helpful in the recruiting process.

Materials Tracking
To help you keep track of all the information you are sending coaches, I suggest you make up a materials tracking sheet so that you are well organized. I have provided a sample sheet on the next page.

Calls
I would advise that you call a coach before you are sending the above information and after you have sent it. After that the coach will call you and contact you if he or she is interested.

Tracking Sheet

School _ABC University_

Coach _Bob Smith_

Phone Number _(555) 555-5555_

Email _coach@abcu.edu_

Notes _Sent info on Jan. 15. Need to call Feb. 1 to follow up._

Parent or Athlete

I am often asked who should be the one making these phone calls, the student-athlete or parent. As a coach, personally I like talking to both the kid and parent. I do not like to see parents who constantly handle all communication for their kids, for several reasons. First off, it does not show much in the way of maturity. By the time one is a high school senior, they should feel comfortable talking on the phone, even to college coaches. Parents can start the call or ask their own questions, but certainly not do all the talking. When it comes to scheduling visits, getting directions, or discussing financial aid, most coaches expect to talk to a parent.

CHAPTER FIVE

ELIGIBILITY & RECRUITING RULES

After using the method described in the previous chapter, you will have one of two situations. You will be or not be recruited by the coach. If you are recruited, you will either get a personal letter (see sample), questionnaire (sample), or phone call from the coach. If you are being recruited, congratulations, your objectives have been met. Feel free to send me more money if you'd like :-)

If you do not hear from the coach or you receive a letter stating that you will not be recruited (sample), there is little that you can do. If you are not recruited by a coach, but still want to attend that school and tryout for the team, that is your right. In this case, you would be considered a walk-on. Walk-ons have had many success stories. Many have gone on to star in college programs. Of course, others have been cut after a day of tryouts. The best thing you can do if you choose to walk-on is to notify the coach that you are doing so. Coaches are much more likely to give you an adequate tryout if they know who you are and that you will be trying out. If someone just shows up to try out, they must really star to be given a shot. Keep in mind that with the effects of Title IX, the days of walk-ons and JV teams are almost gone. Team rosters need to be as lean as possible at most schools and thus, there is not the extra room to develop players as there was in the past. For this reason, walking on is tougher then ever. Don't be misled when you watch Division I football on TV and hear an announcer talk about a star player who was a walk-on as a freshman. When you play at that level, a walk on simply means a player who did not get a scholarship as opposed to a player the coach never heard of who made the team. Since Division I football has 85 scholarships, the majority of the people on the team are receiving one.

If the coach is not interested in recruiting you, it would be helpful to find out why. There is nothing wrong with calling to ask the coach why he or she is not interested. Maybe they think you would be better of in a less competitive program. Maybe it is your academic ability. Perhaps they do not need your particular event or position for a few years. Regardless, it will help you with your search effort to know why the coach has passed on you.

Sample Return Letter From Coach

Mr. All-League Goalie
Shot Stopping Lane
Save, CA 90025

Dear Athlete,

Thank you for taking the time to inquire more about the soccer program at ABC University. I appreciate your interest in both our institution and strong soccer program.

From the information you have provided, it appears you are the type of student who would excel at ABC U. For this reason, I have enclosed some information that highlights our many academic programs. Please don't hesitate to contact me should you need more specific information.

I am hopeful you will continue to investigate our institution. The resources available to our students, including full access to our recently constructed sports center, have set the stage for the future. We are hopeful you will be a part of ABC U and our men's soccer program!

We will be staying in touch.

Sincerely,

Wayne Mazzoni
Head Men's Soccer Coach
ABC University

Sample Questionnaire

ABC University
Women's Basketball, Student-Athlete Questionnaire

Name_____

PSAT: Date_____ V:_____ M:_____

Address_____

SAT: Date_____ V:_____ M:_____

City_____ State_____ ZIP_____

ACT: Date_____ V:_____ M:_____

Home Phone_____ Class Rank_____ of ____ GPA_____

Social Security #_____ D.O.B._____

Graduation Date_____ Counselor_____

Intended Major_____

CareerGoal_____

Father_____ Occupation_____

High School_____

Mother_____ Occupation_____

High School_____

Address_____ City_____

State_____ Zip_____ Phone_____

HT_____ WT_____ Vertical Leap_____ Position_____

Points Per Game: FR_____ SO_____ JR_____

FG%:   FR_____ SO_____ JR_____

Assists/Game: FR_____ SO_____ JR_____

Steals: FR_____ SO_____ JR_____

Rebounds/Game: FR_____ SO_____ JR_____

FT%:   FR_____ SO_____ JR_____

AthleticHonors_____

H.S. Coach School Phone_____ Home Phone_____

Return To: ABC U, Women's Basketball
Phone: (999) 555-1357, Sportstown, ST 12343-3211

Sample Return Rejection Letter From Coach

ABC University
Men's Lacrosse

September 15, 2003

Mr. Joe Defense
12 Long Stick Lane
Crushem, CO 40054

Dear Athlete,

Thank you very much for your interest in ABC U and the men's lacrosse program. However, I do not feel we make an adequate match. (Or, I do not feel your athletic skills are at the level of our program.)

As you may know, our academic standards have been rising the past several years and your academic performance does not match the guidelines of our admissions department. For this reason, we will not be pursuing you as a student-athlete. Should you continue to decide to apply to the school, we wish you all the best in your admission process.

Should you decide not to continue your efforts at ABC U, I wish you the best in all your endeavors.

Sincerely,

Wayne Mazzoni
Head Men's LAX Coach

Eligibility

The following information is taken from the NCAA Guide for the College Bound Student-Athlete. Copies can be obtained by calling the NCAA at 913.339.1906. There is a hotline at 800.638.3731. The web address is www.ncaa.org.

If you are being recruited, congratulations. As the recruiting process begins, there are several issues of concern. First is your academic eligibility. The NCAA has guidelines to monitor the academic eligibility of high school athletes.

To be what is called a Division I qualifier, that is, someone who is eligible to receive a scholarship, practice, and compete with the team, the following characteristics must be met:

- You must graduate from high school; and,
- Successfully complete a core curriculum of at least 13 academic courses (at least four years in English, two in math, one of year of algebra and one year of geometry (or one year of a higher-level math course for which geometry is a prerequisite), two in social science, two in natural or physical science (including at least one lab class, if offered by your high school); one additional course in English, math or natural or physical science; and two additional academic courses (which may be taken from the already-mentioned categories, e.g., foreign language, computer science, philosophy)).
  Note: Each individual high school has a list of which courses qualify for the NCAA.
- Have a GPA (on the 4.000 max. scale) and a combined score on the SAT verbal and math sections or a sum score on the ACT based on the following qualifier index scale;

QUALIFIER INDEX

Core GPA	ACT	SAT
2.5 & Up	68	820
2.475	69	830
2.450	70	840-850
2.425	70	860
2.400	71	860
2.375	72	870
2.350	73	880
2.325	74	890
2.300	75	900
2.275	76	910
2.250	77	920
2.225	78	930
2.200	79	940
2.175	80	950
2.150	80	960
2.125	81	960
2.100	82	970
2.075	83	980
2.050	84	990
2.025	85	1000
2.000	86	1010

Partial Qualifier Index

A partial qualifier cannot compete in contests or events, but is eligible to practice with a team at its home facility and receive an athletics scholarship during his or her first year at a Division I school and then has three seasons of competition. A partial qualifier may play a fourth year, if the beginning of the fifth academic years following the students initial, full-time collegiate enrollment, the student has received a baccalaureate degree.

A partial qualifier has not met the requirements of a qualifier, but is required to graduate from high school and meet the index scale on the next page.

PARTIAL QUALIFIER INDEX

Core GPA	ACT	SAT
2.750 & Up	59	720
2.725	59	730
2.700	60	730
2.675	61	740-750
2.650	62	760
2.625	63	770
2.600	64	780
2.575	65	790
2.550	66	800
2.525	67	810

Division II

In Division II, the qualifier requirements are;

- A qualifier must be a high school graduate.
- Have a GPA of 2.000 (on max. 4.000) in 13 core classes (three years of English, two of math, two in social science, two in natural or physical science (at least one lab class, if offered by the school) and two additional courses in English, math or natural science; and two additional academic curses (which may be taken form the already-mentioned categories, e.g., foreign language, computer science, philosophy)).
- Have a combined score on the SAT verbal and math sections of 700 (if taken before April 1, 1995), or 820 (if taken after April 1, 1995), or a 68 sum score on the ACT.

A partial qualifier must graduate from high school and meet one of the following requirements:

- The specified minimum SAT or ACT score; or
- Successful completion of a required core curriculum consisting of a minimum number of course and a specified minimum GPA in the core curriculum.

Division III

These requirements currently do not apply to Division III colleges, where eligibility for financial aid, practice and competition is governed by institutional, conference and other NCAA regulations.

NCAA Clearinghouse

Now, as you will learn, if you have not already, the NCAA has many, many rules which constantly change. A system has been created to handle eligibility issues. It is called the NCAA Initial-Eligibility Clearinghouse for Division I and II. YOU MUST REGISTER WITH THE CLEARINGHOUSE IF YOU PLAN TO PARTICIPATE AS A COLLEGE FRESHMAN. Did I make that point loud enough? Do not get burned by the system. Even with the NCAA Clearinghouse there have still been eligibility problems. Hundreds of students each year are not able to play because of some complication. Stories in many papers, including The New York Times, have covered such cases. Your high school guidance counselors should know all about this process. As of 2002 you must file this paperwork online. Go to www.ncaa.org to file. Counselors can obtain registration materials, at no cost, by calling the clearinghouse at 319.337.1492. Take care of this issue early. The best time is after your junior-year grades appear on your transcript. If you have any additional problems, call the NCAA Clearinghouse at 319.339.3003.

Recruiting Rules

As defined by the NCAA, you become a "prospective student-athlete" when you start ninth-grade classes. Before the ninth grade, you become a prospective student-athlete if a college gives you (or your relatives or friends) any financial aid or other benefits that the college does not provide to prospective students generally.

You become a "recruited prospective student-athlete" at a particular college if any coach or representative of the college's athletic interests (booster or representative) approaches you (or any member of your family) about enrolling and participating in athletic at that college. Activities by coaches or boosters that cause you to become a recruited prospective student athlete are:

- Providing you with an official visit;
- Placing more than one telephone call to you or any other member of your family; or
- Visiting you or any other member of your family anywhere other than on the college's campus.

There are many recruiting rules to be aware of concerning phone calls, contacts, evaluations, official visits, and printed materials sent. It is advisable to call the NCAA for the guide and be familiar with rules. Coaches are required to know the rules and in fact are tested and regulated by the NCAA. However, improper recruiting will not only hurt the coach and school, it will hurt your opportunities as well.

Campus Visits
An Official Visit is paid for by the school. However, it comes with certain rules:

- You can have an official visit only once at each school and can receive no more than five such visits (even if you are being recruited for different sports).
- This visit cannot be taken unless you have given the college your high school transcript and a score from a PSAT, SAT or PACT Plus or ACT.
- Expenses can be paid by the school for you and your parents or legal guardian, but no one else.
- You cannot stay on campus for more than forty-eight hours.
- You may receive meals, lodging, and complimentary admissions to campus athletic contests (tickets must be general seating).
- A coach may only accompany you on your official visit when the transportation occurs by automobile and all transportation occurs within the 48-hour period.
- Meals provided to you (and/or your parents) on an official visit may be provided either on or off the institution's campus.
- In addition, a student host may help you become acquainted with campus life. The host may spend $30 per day to cover all costs of entertaining you. However, the money can't be used to purchase souvenirs such as T-shirts or other college mementos.

It is wise to review the basic rules so that when the time comes for you to play you are eligible.

> *The best advice on this subject is to get the best grades you can, starting in ninth grade, all the way through your senior year. If you do this, all the eligibility and clearinghouse issues will be taken care of.*

CHAPTER SIX

QUESTIONS TO ASK THE COACH

Athletes are often so excited to be recruited that they never get answers to questions that would have saved them heartache after they enrolled. They have a view of reality about certain things at the college level. If only they would have given these issues some thought and gotten the necessary answers.

The following are items most athletes never consider:

- Is there an off-season program? What is it? How extensive? Must you play in the off-season? You should know what your commitment will entail as well as what opportunities there are to better yourself. If there is litle that you can do in the off-season how do you expect to improve and get more playing time or make it to the next level.

- Can I play two sports? Some programs will not allow you to, yet some are fine. But clearly this is something you will want to know in advance.

- What are the practice and game facilities like? This is important if you are concerned or want to compare schools based on their practice and game facilities. One student I know attended a college for baseball, only to realize there was no field on campus and that they had to take a half-hour bus ride everyday. Keep in mind that the best facilities often attract the best athletes. This is fine if you are one of those athletes. If not, you may wind up going to a school since you love the basketball court, but are not talented enough to get on that floor during a game.

• How about off-season facilities? Oftentimes teams that are not in-season are stuck with space problems for practice, especially in the colder climates. Not every school may have sufficient facilities and your off-season development could be limited

• What kinds of exercise facilities are there? Weight room, equipment, space. If you are looking to develop yourself physically, it helps to have adequate equipment

• Are there any plans for future building or equipment? Today is the age of facility development. Schools which have little at the present time, could have plans to build a state of the art facility in the near future

• Is there an equipment manager who handles practice and game laundry or will that be left up to you? Not every college has such a person. If this matters to you, check it out. In addition, what items will be provided for you. Certain programs provide sneakers, cleats, etc.

• What was the team's record last year? What is the outlook this year? Do you want to play in a program that is already winning? Do you like the challenge of helping a program improve? It is up to you and of course, your talent level.

• What percentage of the team receives a full scholarship? A partial scholarship? A recruited player receiving no scholarship money? Walk-on? More on this later.

- Have any players gone on to play professionally? If this is your aspiration, it would help to know if the program has turned out any professionals.

- What is the schedule like? How many games or matches? What is the strength of the opponents?

- How will my schoolwork be affected? Or, how many hours per day in-season will my sport take? Sports such as baseball require lots of travel. How much class will be missed and how the coach and professors handle that is of the utmost importance. What do you do when you have a conflict between class and practice or a game?

- Is there a J.V., Freshman, or "B" team? It is good to know if you will have a chance to develop should you not make varsity right away.

- Will games interfere with your program of study? If you are a pre-med. major and have three labs a week in the afternoon, this could be a problem, can anything be done now to solve it.

- Are there many overnight stays? Again relating to classes.

- Are there any nationally ranked opponents on the schedule? This may be relevant if you like a challenge and if you want media attention.

- Will any games be on radio or TV? What about the press coverage? This might be of concern to you because it would be great to be on TV or in the paper or it could help your exposure as an athlete.

- What is the coach's reputation? Is she/he new or experienced? Does she/he have a local or national reputation? Is she/he the type of coach you would like? How long has she/he been at the school? The best person to give you feedback about the coach are the players now on the team. Parents of current players are a good source as well.

- What do current and former players think about the coach? Ask as many players as you can. Not everyone will like or dislike the coach, but hearing opinions is important to see if you mesh with the coaches' style.

- What do the parents of current players think? Parents usually know all the details about the team. Ask them.

- What is the coaches' style or philosophy? In terms of personality, character, morals, etc.

- What style of offense or defense, etc. do they use? Does it suit you? If you are a quarterback who is much better in a pro style dropback offense, it would serve you well to know which teams run the wishbone.

- What are the assistant coaches like? You will be interacting with assistants a lot. What are they like? What if one of them became head coach?

- Who is ahead of you at your desired position? How many? How good? What year? If the freshman at your position was an All-American you might want to consider another program, unless you believe you can beat him or her out.

- How many people will be brought in at my position? If you play left wing on a hockey team and the coach has recruited nine left wings, this may be of concern.

- What role does the coach see you playing? What is her assessment of your ability? Beware of the college coach who offers you the starting position before you beat out the existing player. If she does it to her current player, she could do it to you.

- Does the coach plan to red-shirt you? What is your feeling if the answer is yes? Red shirting happens at most of the bigger programs. The idea is that you are more likely to help the team as a fifth year senior then you are as a young freshman. This is also time to adjust to school, learn the game at the next level and prepare for your future years. Big question…who pays for the fifth year?

- What is the personality of players on the team? Are they similar to you? Do they play to win or just to play? Are academics important to them? Could they be your friends for life?

- If you are offered a scholarship, what happens if you are hurt or declared ineligible for any reason?

- If you are in academic trouble, what will the coach do to help? Some programs have academic counseling department already created to help in these situations.

- What happens if you get hurt? Does the school have an insurance policy that covers you? What doctors can you use? Important information.

- If you are hurt, who determines if you are ready again for competition? Is it a doctor, trainer or the coach?

- Are drugs a problem on campus? On the team?

- What is the team budget? Are you required to raise money for team expenses? Do you pay for extra equipment or can the budget provide for such expenses? Can the budget handle a championship season. What about travel and accommodations? Do you sleep ten to a room and take buses across the country for away games?

- What is the graduation rate of athletes? What is the team GPA? Do athletes have a study hall? Are tutors available? This shows the emphasis on academics.

- Is the team active in the community? This can help for your resume, networking for jobs, and simply doing something for others.

- What kind of support is there from the student body and local community? Do you care if nine or 90,000 people attend games.

As you can see from reading the questions, they are very important to your four years. Not all questions may concern you, but I am sure some do. Don't be embarrassed to ask questions. If this were a job interview, you would have questions for your employer. (Is there a lot of travel in the job? What are my chances of moving up within the organization? etc.)

Other things that will help you decide if the situation is good are to observe games and practices. See how the players and coaches get along and notice the level or seriousness and intensity. Ask players on the team why they chose the school and if they aren't playing, why they stay. Get a schedule and press guide. Check out the competition and background of players.

Further, it is important to see if the coach speaks positively or negatively of other schools, programs or coaches. The respectful coach will say nothing or only positive things about other schools.

Recruiting is a two way street. You don't have to beg to play college athletics. Get the necessary information. Coaches do not mind answering questions about themselves, their programs, and their goals. If they do, they are either covering up something or they do not wish to spend the time with your concerns.

Again, it is so important to ask questions because your assumptions may be incorrect. For example, what if you played two sports your whole life and planned to do so in college, only to find out that your coach demands you practice with the team in the off-season or you will lose your scholarship? It never hurts to ask. Don't be shy.

Don't hurt your college athletic career because you were too afraid to ask. If you were buying a house, you would have it inspected; buying a car, you read the ratings or take it to a mechanic; and before accepting a job, you would have many questions. Recruiting is the same. Ask questions.

CHAPTER SEVEN

MAXIMIZING CHANCES OF GETTING ACCEPTED

Now that you have done everything possible to narrow down colleges and to be known by the coaches you want, it is time to get going with the applications. This section will shed light on what coaches, and more importantly, admissions departments, are looking for from applicants. I will also explain how you can use athletics and other contacts to help you get into a college or university.

Early Decision

The single best way to get into the college of your choice is to apply under early decision. However, this takes efficient work and some risk. Applying early requires several things. First, you must be decisive enough to know, in the first semester of your senior year, which college you want to attend. If you apply early and are accepted, you must attend that college.

You have a better chance of getting in this way because all admissions departments are seeking two things: filling the class and getting as many good applicants as possible. By having many good applicants to a school, admissions offices can be more selective and the ranking of the school goes up. Harvard University takes 60% of its class from the early pool of applicants.

Again, applying early raises your chances of getting in. In fact, schools like to know that you think so highly of them that you are willing to go "cut throat." Think about it, if someone asked you and ten other people for a date, you are likely to decline. (Unless of course he/she is really attractive!) But, if that person asks only you, you are likely to feel more special and more inclined to say yes. You must, of course, be close to the admissions criteria, but more slack is allowed at this time. Some schools won't accept you right away, but hold your application for the spring "pool."

In terms of the application process, admissions departments have several criteria they use to evaluate potential students. Some weigh the factors more heavily than others.

The list is as follows:

A New York Times magazine study showed that Harvard takes more then half of it's freshmen class from early decision

GPA

GPA is very important because serves as an indicator of your academic performance. Further, a high board score and a low GPA will show that you are smart but not a hard worker.

A poor GPA will limit the colleges that are available to you. Thus, if you still have time to raise your grades, it is advisable to hit the books.

In addition, don't rest on SAT scores as your way to get accepted. If you scored 1400 on your SAT's, but have a 2.1 GPA, you will be labeled smart, but lazy and may not have the pick of schools you could have.

Class Rank

Your class rank (if your school does this) is important because this tells the admissions department where you fit into you class. If the department is making a decision on two students with similar applications from the same school, and choose to accept the one who is say, 150/500, then most likely they will accept the person who is 85/500.

Strength of High School

The rating of your high school will be a concern to colleges. High schools are all ranked by difficulty and while there is not much you can do about this, just beware that it does exist. While I would not advise anyone to transfer high schools for this reason, some have done it.

Classes Taken

The types and strength of classes taken is considered. Stronger classes obviously make a favorable impression and may "excuse" you in part for a relatively low GPA. Any Advanced Placement or college level courses help immensely.

If your transcript is really unimpressive you might consider attending a summer school session offered by some colleges.

Extracurricular Activities

Activities you participated in, such as sports, community efforts, and any awards you won are an important source of application information. Colleges feel that students who do more than just their schoolwork are more likely to add to the life of the campus. In addition, all schools hope to produce alumni who give the school positive recognition, and this is often done by hard working over achievers.

SAT/ACT Scores

While most colleges attempt to say that the scores from these standardized test are weighed with equal value to other factors, it is my belief, for better or worse, that they are often the chief criteria. SAT scores mean rankings for colleges and are important for a schools reputation. Taking a preparation course is much advised. Keep in mind that a high SAT score is as often due to test-taking skills as it is to intelligence.

If you and your family have the time and money to invest in test prep classes, this is clearly money well spent. Colleges make decisions off this test. Do as well as you can.

Interview

Similar to the job interview you will have in a few years (so enjoy college while you can!) the interview is of the utmost importance. Many students never even make the effort to have an interview. Again, while the lack of an interview is not supposed to hurt your chances, I believe a solid interview is the clincher. Schedule an interview, relax and be yourself. If you don't look good on paper, use this opportunity to convince the admissions committee of your qualities.

Questions from Admissions Counselors:

1. What do you like most about high school?
2. What do you like least?
3. Why are you interested in this college?
4. What other schools are you looking at?
5. What are you looking for in a school?
6. What do you intend to study?
7. What are your career goals?
8. What extracurricular activities do you participate in?
9. What will you add to this campus?
10. If someone were reading your eulogy what would they say about you?
11. What would your friends say about you?
12. What would your teachers say about you?
13. Whom do you most admire?
14. If you could meet three famous people, who would they be and why?
15. Do you plan to join the Greek system?
16. Can you explain your low GPA? SAT? Class Rank? Hopefully, they don't ask you all these :-(
17. Tell me about a time in your life when you overcame a major obstacle?
18. What are your biggest strengths and weaknesses?
19. What are you most proud of?
20. Do you plan to play collegiate sports?
21. What activities would you want to be involved in on campus?
22. Do you know any alumni? What did they tell you about the school?

23. What does college mean to you?
24. Tell me why you should be admitted?

Questions for Admissions Counselors:

1. What are the graduation rates for athletes? Non-athletes?
2. How long does it take the average person to graduate?
3. What is the placement rate and average starting salary of graduates in your field of study?
4. Is there a network for alumni to help graduating students?
5. What is the financial aid policy? Am I eligible?
6. What programs are in place to help if I am having trouble in a class?
7. What are the major additions or changes taking place in the next four years?
8. Will it be easier for me to be accepted into the graduate school on campus because
I attended undergraduate school here?

Keep in mind that many of the interviewers are themselves graduates of the school you are applying to, so feel free to ask them how they liked it.

When visiting with a college coach or admissions counselor, don't just be a bump on a log. Be outgoing, enthusiastic. Ask questions, interact, have fun. They are people too.

Application and Essay

Your application is very important and should be done thoroughly and neatly. Have your guidance department look over all the materials before they are sent out.

Your essay is crucial as well. This is your chance to shine, make the best of it. Practice it and write it several times before you put it on the application for good. Have it proofread by as many people as you can. If you have had a major achievement or overcome some problem, it makes for a great story. In my coaching days, I was told that one of my recruits wrote an application that brought the admissions counselor to tears. It came from the heart and helped him get accepted.

As many colleges try to assemble a "diverse" student body, bring to their attention any exotic details from you background.

Educational Consultants

There are people who help you with the application and essay procedure called educational consultants. They are people who have extensive experience in the guidance or admissions department of high schools or colleges. If you can afford one, it can only help.

Letters of Recommendation

You will be asked to submit letters of recommendation, which believe me, are read. Try to obtain these from teachers, employers, coaches, etc. who know you relatively well.

Connections

The "legacy" system favors admissions for applicants whose relatives attended the school. Additionally, it helps to know someone who is in any way associated with the college (professor, coach, member of admissions committee!).

If possible get a letter from anyone that has a connection with the school. This may take some research, but a phone call or letter from a current or former student, faculty or staff member will put you ahead of the rest. Admission people want to know that someone who knows what their school is about and what you're about, think you make a match.

Coach's Request

Coaches at schools have varying degrees of influence with the admissions department. At certain schools, if the coach wants a player, she is in. At others, the coach has less power. Regardless, coaches can only help you be accepted.

Many schools have a procedure that allows coaches to select the few student-athletes whom they really want to be accepted. This usually takes place in the form of an Expression of Interest (EOI) sheet. This is a personal letter from the coach, often read by the dean of admissions and even the school president, stating reasons why this person should be accepted. They don't work every time, but they very often do.

Now that you are aware of what schools are looking for from their applicants you can take the necessary steps to set yourself apart from the crowd.

Now, no book, organization, or person can promise anyone an athletic scholarship (and beware if they do!), however there are some clear-cut ways to learn what moneys are available.

CHAPTER EIGHT

MAXIMIZING SCHOLARSHIP POTENTIAL

Each year there are over 100,000 scholarships available in Division I and II (not including community and junior colleges) worth over $500,000,000. Here's how you can get a piece of that.

You Have Got to Ask

The first key factor in obtaining scholarship offers is to ask about available money. If the player does not mention money, then the coach may simply assume the family has sufficiently means and does not need help with tuition. This is not a job interview where the subject of money must come up because you are getting paid for your services. In college athletics you can play for free or they can pay you to play, but you must ask!

The Questions

Back to scholarship issues. The way you can introduce the topic of scholarships to a coach is by asking the following questions:

- How many players receive full scholarships?
- How many players receive partial scholarships?

- How many are available for this season?
- What are your recruiting needs?
- What is your opinion of my scholarship value with your team?

This is just a way to get the initial read from te coach. You will get a response indicating that you are:

- A full scholarship athlete.
- A partial scholarship athlete. To which you can ask for an estimated dollar figure.
- They are unsure of what to offer you because they are still recruiting other athletes.
- They don't see you as a scholarship athlete.

If you are offered a full scholarship, congratulations.

If you are offered a partial scholarship find out the amount and wait to hear from other schools. Remember that coaches can take a scholarship and divide it any way they like. For example, if a particular sport has ten scholarship to offer and the cost of tuition, room, books, and boarding for one year is $20,000, then they have $200,000 in scholarship money available. They can give ten people full scholarships, or 20 people half scholarships ($10,000). Alternatively, they offer someone $4,356.22 if they like. This is why there is room to bargain and negotiate.

In most Division I and II schools, scholarships are equivalency scholarships. This means that if a school has ten scholarships worth $200,000, like in the above example, they can give the money out to as many athletes as they like. Thus, they could give ten full scholarships worth $20,000 or five full and ten partial. Any combination is possible as long as they don't exceed the maximum number allowed in their sport.

Scholarships Offered Men's Division I / Division II

SPORT	DIVISION I	DIVISION II
Baseball	11.7	9.0
Basketball	13	10.0
Cross-Country/Track	12.6	12.6
Fencing	4.5	4.5
Football	85 (63 FOR IAA)	36.0
Golf	4.5	3.6
Gymnastics	6.3	5.4
Ice Hockey	18.0	13.5
Lacrosse	12.6	10.8
Rifle	3.6	
Skiing	6.3	6.3
Soccer	9.9	9.0
Swimming	9.9	8.1
Tennis	4.5	4.5
Volleyball	4.5	4.5
Water Polo	4.5	4.5
Wresting	9.9	9.0

Scholarships Offered Women's Division I / Division II

SPORT	DIVISION I	DIVISION II
Archery	9.0	9.0
Badminton	10.0	10.0
Basketball	15.0	10.0
Bowling	5.0	5.0
Cross Country/Track	16.0	12.6
Fencing	5.0	4.5
Field Hockey	11.0	6.3
Golf	5.0	5.4
Gymnastics	10.0	6.0
Ice Hockey	18.0	18.0
Lacrosse	11.0	9.9
Rowing	20.0	20.0
Skiing	7.0	6.3
Soccer	11.0	9.9
Softball	11.0	7.2
Squash	9.0	9.0
Swimming	14.0	8.1
Synch. Swimming	5.0	5.0
Team Handball	12.0	12.0
Tennis	8.0	6.0
Volleyball	12.0	8.0
Water Polo	8.0	8.0

It is important to note that the above chart shows the maximum scholarship amounts allowed by the NCAA. It is normal for a school to offer less than the maximum due to budget restrictions.

In Division I men's basketball and football, as well as Division I women's tennis, volleyball and gymnastics the scholarship are a head count. For example, Division I football has 85 scholarships. The maximum number of players receiving a scholarship is 85, whether or not they are full scholarships.

If you are not offered any money, it doesn't necessarily mean they don't want you. There may be no money available for this season or it was spent on other top recruits. However, if you have your heart set on playing at that school, ask the coach's opinion of your ability. If the coach want you on the team but can't offer you a scholarship you would be a recruited non-scholarship player. Thus, you still know you have a chance to play, but without financial assistance.

In other situations, you would be a true walk on player. This means that not only is there no money available for you, but that you must take your chances to make the team.

When the discussion of money is brought up, you should also ask the coach if there are any special endowments or other scholarships available to people from certain background. Often former alumni or other individuals will contribute money to people of specific backgrounds. It doesn't hurt to ask.

Money Early and Late

Now a key issue for scholarship money, and I encourage you to read this closely, is that there is money available early in the recruiting process, and often very late, in the recruiting process. The reason for this is as follows. Let us say, for example, that a coach has $50,000 to offer athletes for the upcoming season. If the school costs $20,000 and he offers two athletes scholarships and they accept right away, then there is $10,000 remaining.

A coach may offer this money to one recruit who is waiting for other schools to make their offers. If that player decides to choose another program, then there is $10,000 waiting to be spent. Oftentimes all the best players have already accepted, so coaches give this money to players in the middle ability area.

To get the coaches best and final offer there are several things you can do. First, make him aware of other offers you are receiving. If a similar program is offering you $10,000, they may feel you are worth that to them as well. It is ill-advised to lie about these matters, because coaches have a way of finding out.

It's A Negotiation Process

In addition, if you have been offered a partial scholarship you can use the above process to ask for more money, in hopes that there will be some left over at the end. Always remember that scholarships are not given out in blocks. Coaches have certain amounts available for the year. If they want to give you $8,372.23, they can.

Thus, if they offer you $5,000, always ask if they can do a little better, especially if you're ready to close the deal. You could say, "Coach, I'd love to play for you and your school, a little more money would make the deal right now." It often works. Especially when your parents really can't afford the tuition. Make sure the coach knows the money will be a deciding factor.

National Letter of Intent

An athletic scholarship comes in the form of a National Letter of Intent. In essence this is a form that binds you to go to the school that sent it. If you have ever seen the news where a star high school prospect is seen signing an agreement to go to a particular college, this is the form he or she is signing. Do not sign or send this form unless you are certain of your choice. One of the biggest questions asked by high school athletes and their parents is whether or not a scholarship is for all four years. There answer is no. A scholarship is a one- year agreement. A coach can give or take additional money year by year. However, it is rarely done. A coach does not want the reputation of taking away a player's scholarship. This will only hurt him or her in recruiting other players. However, should you get a scholarship and quit the team, you will no longer receive and athletic money.

CHAPTER NINE

MAKING THE FINAL DECISION

Once you have been accepted or rejected (hopefully not from to many) from the schools to which you applied, it is time to make the final decision. Often this can be the most agonizing part. It is when you start to realize that this one decision will affect the rest of your life. For most, this is the biggest decision you have made to date. So here is some advice to make it a little easier.

Decision Chart
You must take into account all the factors from the above sections. Such as student body, size, location, climate, appearance of campus, etc. This can best be done on a Matrix chart, whereby you weigh each factor by its importance to you

Academic Reputation
However, if after you do this and all the schools still feel equal, there is only one thing to do. In my opinion you should give the most consideration to the school that has the best academic reputation, where you can participate in athletics.

The reasoning behind this stems from the fact that once you are in college, most schools are equally difficult as far as the class work. Now this is not to say the Ivy League is similar to a community college, but I assume students who are accepted into schools are not choosing between such extremes. Thus, in schools of similar characteristics, pick the best academic school.

VALUES CHART FOR MAKING THE FINAL CHOICE

FACTOR	WEIGHT (1-5)	SCHOOL 1	SCHOOL 2	SCHOOL 3
Location	4	4 = 16	3 = 12	5 = 20
Setting	3	2 = 6	3 = 9	4 = 12
Academics	5	5 = 25	4 = 20	4 = 20
Cost	4	1 = 4	3 = 12	5 = 20
Size	3	2 = 6	3 = 9	3 = 9
Campus	3	5 = 15	3 = 9	4 = 12
Faculty/Major	2	3 = 6	4 = 8	3 = 6
Athletics	4	3 = 12	4 = 12	5 = 20
Other	3	3 = 9	3 = 9	3 = 9
Total		99	100	128

Money Talks

Another factor may influence your decision: the amount of financial aid from all sources. Whether it be scholarships, loans, grants or any other source of money, it does play a role in your decision.

Using Your Gut & Campus Visits

If you are still undecided as to your selection using all the above ideas, there is but one thing to do. Use your gut instinct. To have the best information for this gut decision, it is advisable to spend time on campus. Whether you are alone, with friends or family, or an athlete on the team you are hoping to play for, spending time on campus helps you make a more informed decision.

I suggest staying long enough to go to a few classes, a sporting event, and a social gathering to get the full feel. You could also check out the dorms, cafeteria or any other area that concerns you.

As covered earlier if the school pays for your visit, it is an Official Visit of which you are limited to five. However, on an Unofficial Visit, you pay your own way and may make an unlimited number of visits.

If at this point you are still confused, let me ease your mind by saying that if your decision is that close between two schools, either one you choose will be a good choice.

CONCLUSION

The Process Reviewed

Now that we have reached the end of the college selection process, it's time for a quick recap. You first step is to choose colleges that meet non-athletic criteria, such as location and size. Next, these schools are evaluated for their athletic programs and what matches your goals and skills. Third, you make yourself known to these coaches by a clear set of procedures. Coaches will then either recruit you or not recruit you. You must then make sure you are academically eligible and understand recruiting rules so that you do not violate any. Next, you try to do everything possible to be accepted into the schools of your choice. If you are being recruited and are accepted, you must find out if any scholarship money is available to you. Finally, after all this you will be left with choosing the one school that is best for you.

The Process

NARROW YOUR COLLEGES BASED ON ALL FACTORS <u>EXCEPT</u> ATHLETICS. (This can be done as a sophomore, junior, or senior).

Major/Faculty:
- If you know what you want to study, do they have your major?
- Is it a program that would suit you?

Location:
- Do you want to be closer or further from home?
- Do you like a rural or urban setting?

Size:
- Are you looking for a smaller or bigger school?
- Do you need a big name college?

Environment:
- Do you like the campus?
- Does it fit your personality?
- What is the social life like?

> *The best way to determine what you want is by visiting local colleges. This will give you framework for your likes and dislikes.*

LIST 5-20 COLLEGES THAT YOU THINK MEET YOUR NEEDS BASED ON YOUR DESIRES.

1. _____

2. _____

3. _____

4. _____

5. _____

6. _____

7. _____

8. _____

9. _____

10. _____

11. _____

12. _____

13. _____

14. _____

15. _____

16. _____

17. _____

NARROW DOWN YOUR LIST BASED ON YOUR ATHLETIC TALENT LEVEL.

Coaches:
- What level does your high school coach feel you can play?
- How about summer/travel coach?
- Private instructor?
- College coaches that have seen you?

Players:
- How do you rate on your team? Your high school league? Summer team?
- Do you know any players that played with you that now play in college?
- What do they think of your level?

Camps:
- If you attended a college camp, did they rate you?
- How did you feel you ranked with the group of players at the camp?
- Are you aware of any showcase camps in your area?

Skills:
- How do you compare physically?
- Are you fast, strong, quick?
- Do you have poor, average, outstanding skills?
- How much potential do you still have?

Visits:
- When visiting the college, see if you get a chance to watch the team practice or play.
- There is no better feedback on how you compare then watching the team at the next level.

Circle the levels that you feel are right for you:		
Low Division III	Mid-Level Division III	High Level Division III
Low Division II	Mid-Level Division II	High Level Division II
Low Division I	Mid-Level Division I	High Level Division I

FROM YOUR LIST OF SCHOOLS, WHICH HAVE ATHLETIC PROGRAMS AT THE LEVELS YOU CIRCLED? LIST THE 5-10 THAT FIT.

1. _____   6. _____

2. _____   7. _____ _____

3. _____   8. _____

4. _____   9. _____

5. _____   10. _____

PREPARING YOUR MARKETING PACKAGE
(Check items as you complete them.)

- ☐ Cover Letter
- ☐ Resume
- ☐ Transcripts
- ☐ Board Scores
- ☐ Press Clips
- ☐ Reference Letters
- ☐ Photo
- ☐ Practice Or Game Film
- ☐ Game Schedules
- ☐ Items Copied For All The Schools

TRACK THE MATERIALS YOU SEND AND FOLLOW UP

School _____ Coach _____
Phone Number _____ Email _____
Notes_____

School _____ Coach _____
Phone Number _____ Email _____
Notes_____

School _____ Coach _____
Phone Number _____ Email _____
Notes_____

School _____ Coach _____
Phone Number _____ Email _____
Notes_____

School _____ Coach _____
Phone Number _____ Email _____
Notes_____

School _____ Coach _____
Phone Number _____ Email _____
Notes_____

School _____ Coach _____
Phone Number _____ Email _____
Notes_____

School _____ Coach _____
Phone Number _____ Email _____
Notes_____

School _____ Coach _____
Phone Number _____ Email _____
Notes_____

School _____ Coach _____

Phone Number _____ Email _____

Notes_____

School _____ Coach _____

Phone Number _____ Email _____

Notes_____

School _____ Coach _____

Phone Number _____ Email _____

Notes_____

School _____ Coach _____

Phone Number _____ Email _____

Notes_____

School _____ Coach _____

Phone Number _____ Email _____

Notes_____

School _____ Coach _____

Phone Number _____ Email _____

Notes_____

School _____ Coach _____

Phone Number _____ Email _____

Notes_____

School _____ Coach _____

Phone Number _____ Email _____

Notes_____

School _____ Coach _____

Phone Number _____ Email _____

Notes_____

TRACK SCHOOLS THAT HAVE SHOWN INTEREST

School _____ Visit Date _____
Answers to important questions _____
_____
_____

School _____ Visit Date _____
Answers to important questions _____
_____
_____

School _____ Visit Date _____
Answers to important questions _____
_____
_____

School _____ Visit Date _____
Answers to important questions _____
_____
_____

School _____ Visit Date _____
Answers to important questions _____
_____
_____

School _____ Visit Date _____
Answers to important questions _____
_____
_____

School _____ Visit Date _____
Answers to important questions _____
_____
_____

ADDITIONAL CHECKLIST ITEMS
(Check completed items.)

- ☐ NCAA Clearinghouse
- ☐ Applications
- ☐ Interviews
- ☐ FAFSA Forms

CHART FOR MAKING THE FINAL CHOICE

FACTOR	WEIGHT (1-5)	SCHOOL 1	SCHOOL 2	SCHOOL 3
Location				
Setting				
Academics				
Cost				
Size				
Campus				
Faculty/Major				
Athletics				
Other				
Total				

Prepping for College In the Classroom

From my years as a college student, college teacher, and coach, I have learned several things along the way that can help you both prepare for your new life in college and excel when you are there.

First and foremost is to read. Become an avid reader of the newspaper, magazines, and both fiction and non-fiction books. More then anything else related to academics in college, you will be shocked, and possibly overwhelmed by the amount of reading that you will have to do. Imagine walking into your first semester of classes, usually four or five courses, and getting five chapters assigned in each. Reading, more so than anything else, is the ability to teach yourself new information. Every adult who has a job and is no longer in school reads to learn new information. Whether it be the Internet, watching a video, going to seminars, or reading most professions require you to read. Doctors, lawyers, financial executives, coaches, etc., all must read to keep up to date on what they are doing. Most have to be able to read and comprehend simply to do their jobs on a day-to-day basis. While you were asked to do some reading in high school, the amount you will face in college will flood you if you are not prepared.

As in all of life, if you can practice and improve both your writing and speaking skills this will serve you as well.

Once you are in college there are several things you can do to ensure that you get the best grades possible. Most importantly, go to class. I can all but assure you that if you attend every single class, at the very minimum you will pass. If you go to class awake, showered, dressed well, prepared, sitting in the front row and participating, you are getting closer to an A.

Getting to know your teacher on a more personal basis is well advised. Meeting with them a few times a semester just to talk or ask advice will turn you from a student in class to a real person. If you want to do extremely well ask for extra credit work to do. If you receive a poor grade on an assignment, ask if you can do it over. Remember the squeaky wheel gets the grease.

In the modern day of computers, it is all but a given that your assignments, papers, and presentations should all be done on computer. Handing in work that is hand written, especially if sloppy, will hurt your grade with most professors.

Prepping for College, Athletically

Again from having been a college athlete and coach, I can give you several tips that will help you get off to the best start possible in your sport. First and foremost is to get yourself into peak physical condition. The biggest adjustment most athletes have is not so much in the skill or technique of the sport, but in keeping up with those who are much bigger, stronger, and faster. While most of you played with older athletes at some point during your high school career, the jump in that regard is even greater in college. Most likely you will be entering college at seventeen or eighteen. Right away you will be competing with players who are as old as twenty-three. The amount of time they had to physically mature, as well as workout year round in college will make that gap extremely wide. The more you can narrow it down by being at your peak strength, speed, and skill the better you will be.

Additionally, come into your season in playing shape. Don't expect there to be a grace period, especially as a freshman. If you want to show yourself in the best possible light, you should be in playing shape regardless of your sport. Even if you sport only has off-season fall practice, you certainly want to be in game playing condition right away.

The Best Four Years of Your Life

Ask just about anyone who went to college and they will say it was the best four years of their life. The reasons are simple. Sports, new friends, relationships, learning, activities, etc., make college a great time. While you will have more responsibility then ever in your life, keep it in perspective. When you leave college to start a career and someday a family, you will realize what you thought was desperately important in college, wasn't all that important. While you should strive to be and do your best, keep in mind you are there to have fun as well. Of course, be responsible with fun. As many people have seen firsthand, some people cannot handle the freedom and responsibility that comes with being on their own. Some do not study enough, others party too often and get involved with drugs and alcohol. The last thing I am attempting to do is tell you how to live your life. You are a mature person who has to choose what to do on your own. However, one piece of advice I'd like to give comes from my grandmother and I would like to share it with you. No matter what the situation or circumstance one thing holds true: live life in moderation. That means if you go to a party with alcohol and you choose to drink, drink a couple of drinks, not ten. If you like chocolate, eat a little. Don't try to avoid eating it for months, only to eat ten candy bars in five minutes. If you live your live in moderation, more often than not it will be a good life.

I wish you much luck in your college decision, athletic career, and in life.

Thoughts from College Coaches

I coach a year-round age group club team that participates at the national level. So I attend all the summer regionals, zones and national championships. If there is a great diver out there I'll learn of him/she. Also I'm quite active in US Diving, our national governing body—so again I learn of talent through those contacts. And finally I scan High School All Americans and send them an introductory letter. Divers must be diving at the national age group level and be a great academic student for me to be interested.

- Rick Schavone, Diving Coach, Stanford University

I find out about recruits through letters of interest sent to us, or questionnaires filled out on our web site. Also, I use the Internet to find prospects. Every state has their own golf association or chapter that hosts big events, and I surf those sites frequently to see who is playing well and shooting good numbers. In golf, athletes can get noticed by playing well in big events. Placing high in a state amateur championship, or Jr. amateur championship, placing well in an AJGA event which is the leading Junior tour in the US. Also, playing well and qualifying for a USGA event will get an athlete recognized. I look more at events like these as opposed to 9-hole scores from high school matches. The only high school scores I look at are ones from an 18-hole state championship or regional tournament. Obviously, consistency is very key to being recognized. I want a kid that can go out and shoot 75 everyday of the week, as opposed to a kid who can put up a 71 but follow up with 84. I believe too many potential student athletes rely on their high school scores, and should be getting into more local, state, regional, and national events throughout the summer, and showcasing these on resumes sent to coaches. I'll be interested to see the book when it comes out, and please feel free to use my name in it as needed.

- Todd Howes, Head Men's Golf Coach, Quinnipiac University

At Brown we use 2 National Recruiting services that have been good to us over the years. The services that we use are Collegiate Sports Data and Forbes Report. We also use in state recruiting services coordinated by the High School Coaches Association. The other thing we do is we a send a Recruiting Questionnaire to every High School in the United States. In order to get noticed the first thing I would do return any recruiting questionnaires ASAP (Do not procrastinate). Request the help of your High School Coach in Marketing yourself. If the coach is not as aggressive as you would like seek the help of a parent. In other words do not try to do it yourself. Summer camps are a huge advantage to getting noticed. Do not go to camp for just the name.

When choosing a camp or camps I would look for 2 things: 1. Am I a prospect for this level of football. 2. What are the numbers in the camp. (If I am one of 100 Offensive Lineman am I going to get noticed = Player to Coach Ratio) 3. Will there be any other coaches working the camp. 3) Send out Junior Film Catch the recruiting coaches eyes early. *- Frank Sheehan, Assistant Football Coach, Brown University*

UCONN, being so visible, gets many, many letters of interest. The best kids in swimming simply need to list their time to get noticed. We often go to National level meets to see kids swim. Beyond that, it is just a lot of time. *- Bob Goldberg, Swimming Coach, University of Connecticut.*

The best way for a recruit to get noticed in softball is to get her letters out early during her junior year, even her soph year. Softball coaches do not watch much high school ball at all so summer ball is the way to go. The summer teams should travel to different states for the best tourneys around. ASA is still the way to go around here but Pony is becoming a big organization as well. If a recruit has an interest in a specific school, then she should try to go to that camp during her soph and junior summers. Camp really allows the coaches to get to know the student athlete both on and off the field. Exposure camps are also good but sometime the camps get too big and out of hand, and the college coaches get very frustrated watching them. Personally, we really try to find the athletes who have an interest in us first. Whatever else we see along the way is just extra, and some times it definitely works out. If there is a mutual interest initially - that is the best combination.
- Julie Brzezinski, Head Softball Coach, Fairfield University

I'm a big word of mouth guy, I depend on quality baseball people's opinion. I obviously want to see the kids myself before a scholarship is offered, but we spend a lot of time on the phone talking with HS and JUCO coaches. We also attend the top showcases around the country. I would say that an athlete should try to contact the top 5 universities of his choice at the right time - early in June going into their senior year. From there, he should attend the best showcase events and the camps of the schools of choice. If interested in schools outside his/her area this is crucial. *- Mike Mominey, Head Baseball Coach, Nova Southeastern University*

We review a lot of results from meets, especially the private schools. Summer is big as a lot of athletes are just coming into their own when the HS season ends. Also, we rely heavily on our own athletes to help with kids from their area. *- Ralph White, Men & Women's Track Coach, Williams College.*

The ways we find people that we recruit at Getttysburg is 1. They come to our Top Star recruiting camp at Gettysburg (600 players). 2. We go to other recruiting camps (205, Peak, Champ Camp). 3. - Many players will contact us and we will see films and discuss players with their coaches. 4. - We will see them at a high school game. I really think what a young man can do to get noticed is have a high school coach call and highly recommend a player. For some reason, this really seems to grab my attention. When a coach will verbally commit to a player and highly recommend him. If I get burned by a high school coach once, I will tend not to believe him in the future. - *Hank Janczyk, Men's Lacrosse Coach, Gettysburg College*

We find out about the players we recruit in numerous ways. I would say the most common are the following: prospective players show interest in UC (letter, e-mail, phone call). Recommendation from outside source (high school coach, pro scout, etc.). We see them play during the high school or summer season. Follow high school coverage in newspapers. Scouting recruiting services (which we ignore almost 100% of the time). In each case we try to follow up on any names that we get, but obviously cannot be completely thorough on each name. What we see has more influence than what we hear and some recommenders are more respected than others. With regard to how a player can get noticed, I would suggest that the key is to play in front of as many recruiters as possible. This can be accomplished by playing on a high-level summer team and/or by attending some showcases. I do think that getting seen enough is not as important as being able to display the requisite ability to play at a certain level. A player who does not have the ability to play at a certain level cannot make up for his lack of ability by being seen more. - *Brian Cleary, Head Baseball Coach, University of Cincinnati*

We find players a couple of different ways...through attending high school and summer travel team tournaments—just watching lots of games and lots of teams and through various contacts we have with various high school and travel team coaches around the country. Pittsburgh Softball spends a lot of time in the summer at many local, regional and national tournaments—watching games! A player can best get our attention by sending us a letter of introduction and following that up with a skills video and information about their current schedule. Where can we see them play and when. - *Michelle Phalen, Softball Coach, University of Pittsburgh*

We have several ways of finding out about prospects. We travel to many high-level club tournaments across the country searching for athletes. I subscribe to a couple of recruiting services who provide information about athletes. I truly believe the best way for me to find athletes is by athletes finding us. I receive two dozen or so inquiry letters a week from interested prospects. Each letter gets a response from me and our relationship begins there. As far as high school students getting my attention, beyond pure athleticism, mature, athletes who carry themselves well always draw my attention. I appreciate players who are leaders within their team, on and off the court. I'm as interested in the interaction the athletes have with each other, their coaches, and even their parents, to get a good idea of the type of character they have.

- Chris Ridolfi, Women's Head Volleyball Coach, The College of the Holy Cross

I find out about prospects from letters/profiles/videotapes that they send me, recruiting services, and on-site evaluations by me or my staff at major tournaments. The most important tournaments that we attend are Southern California Kick-Off, Las Vegas Invitational, National Qualifying Tournament, Volleyball Festival, and Junior Nationals. This is how prospects get my attention: 1) If I am watching you play, be an enthusiastic and positive player. Even if you do not have the volleyball skills that we are looking for, we may think that you can contribute to our team if you have the attitude that will bring a spark and energy to our gym. 2) If you are contacting me for the first time, show that you have done your research on the school and make your letter personal (ie, address the letter to me, not just "Coach"). Also, send a profile that describes the type of player and person you are. Things to include are: Contact info; playing experience; positions played; physical descriptors like height, weight, approach jump, reach, block jump; honors; academic info like SAT scores, GPA, AP courses; other extracurricular activities; parent information. 3) If we have been in contact with each other, return messages/correspondence quickly. 4) If you are sending a video, I like to see a short skills portion (3-5 minutes), a short highlight portion (2-3 minutes), and one unedited game in which you are playing well against a good opponent. I will turn the video off when I have seen enough, so don't worry about total length of the video.

- Becky Schmidt Head Volleyball Coach/Asst. Lacrosse Coach, University of Redlands

Typically, I learn of prospects a few different ways. The most common is the student-athlete contacting me. Usually an email from them is the first form of contact. This is the easiest way. Since high schoolers are so great with computers, they get on the web and find schools that have what they're looking for. It's a better situation if the kid says "I want to major in Engineering" and that way they can look up schools that have engineering and the sport they are looking for. The most common problem with all the emails I receive is asking for scholarships. Have the student-athletes do their research first and know what kind of school it is. We are a Division III school which means we don't offer athletic scholarships. We have academic aid, but many of the letters I get ask for information on athletic scholarships. What that also does is puts a bad taste in my mouth, wondering how serious this person is about my program. Another way I identify players is by going out recruiting. If your athletes aren't playing club or select, they will not get the looks they need to by just playing high school. Yes, it's an extra expense, yes it's a lot of traveling, but if there is a talented athlete that is from a 2A high school, major colleges aren't going to look at them. There are exceptions to the rule, though. If you have a pitcher that throws in the 90s consistently, scouts will come and watch. If you have a player like Kobe or Tiger, everyone will know. But, what about those players that aren't as talented as the best player on the team? That just means you have to market yourself that much harder. I grew up in Southern California and played on a very high profile club team, but I still sent out skills tapes and letters. I also got a huge scholarship to a smaller Division I school. I had to shell out $5,000 to go to school for four years, even though it was $18,000 a year. Make sure they send out profile sheets with the following information at the beginning to middle of their junior year: Name, Address (be sure to include the zip code!!!), Email, Phone, GPA, ACT/SAT scores, Class rank, Birthday, SSN, Honors (both academic and athletic), Possible major. Tell your kids that it's a marketing plan! Sell themselves! If they get all-district, send a note to the coaches of the schools they are interested in. Also, if they change club teams or get a different number, let the coaches know! I have watched a player before thinking she was someone else and she didn't fit into my program. It was only later that I realized she had a different number on! Lastly, tell them to be realistic. If you have a female basketball player who loves Uconn and is still wanting to play ball there, but hasn't been getting anything and it's her senior year, look somewhere else. The big schools will hit recruiting hard starting early like in their junior year. They can't speak to them yet, but they will send letters, show up at games, etc. Plus, what is their commitment level? Are they willing to practice 30 hours a week, plus go to school and have a social life? Or is education a number one priority but they still want to play sports? D-III may be a better option.

- Tricia Hoffmann, Head Softball Coach, University of Texas - Dallas

I receive hundreds of letters/e-mails a month from interested student athletes. Not to mention the hundreds of e-mails which come from recruiting services.

The young men who usually make our program, I have heard about from a trusted source (scout, HS coach, etc.) or I have seen play either in person or on video. A player will definitely get my attention if he is not only a solid athlete but a good student as well. HS athletes underestimate the power of doing the job in the classroom. Because if you do, there will be plenty of school's to choose from. - *Scott Laverty, Head Baseball Coach, University of Redlands*

We get many interested student athletes interested in our program. I respond to everyone ho contacts us and write to those I may see at tournaments, club competitions etc. to see if they might be interested in Williams. To get noticed they need to play on a club team that goes to the most competitive tournaments, or ODP competitions. - *MikeRusso, Head Men's Soccer Coach, Williams College*

We watch meet results on the net and keep track of the national swimming federations' databases on athletes. In addition, we find out about swimmers from the current members on the collegiate team. At our university, we have an on-line questionnaire on our website. A swimmers simply fills out the questionnaire and it is forwarded to the swimming office. - *Chuck Knoles, Head Coach Swimming & Diving Coach, University of Pittsburgh*

We do most of our watching at tournaments and via video tape. Because hs and college field hockey seasons run concurrently, it's difficult to get out and see games. If a hs player is interested in our school, her best bet is to be persistent with emails: let us know that she is interested, fill out and return any requested paperwork, videos, etc... update us on her games, set up a visit with admissions, etc.
- *Laura Moliken, Head Field Hockey Coach, Ursinus College*

I make it a point to find out about every basketball team in the state. I study school's classifications; preseason capsules which I find in papers, usually they will list and comment on 6-8 players on a team so I make notes on kids that have size or look for "key" words such as "sleeper", "potential", "keep an eye on" or "major contributor". I will then follow up w/ a standard note and questionnaire to these particular kids. I also try to get to every summer camp in the New England/Tri-state region that I possibly can. Major camps that I hit are Hoop Mountain (Mt. Hermon Prep School in Northfield, MA), Eastern basketball camp (Seton Hall & Coll. of NJ), and 5-star basketball camp (Bryn Mawr, PA or Robert Morris College). I will pay the entrance fee to these camps and they give me a packet of info (recruits name, phone, address etc.). From that point, I evaluate and check off a kid's name who does something on the court that I like. A kid may only do one thing that I like, and I will check his name and send him a form letter and questionnaire. Some characteristics I personally look for: size, attitude, hustle, unselfishness, athleticism (even if its displayed only once during an evaluation), quickness w/ ball, natural instincts, reactions to the ball and to what's happening out on the court, lateral quickness on defense, explosiveness, overall feel for the game (ie: when to make the right play on the court- timing on passes, help defense, shot selection), etc... I like to attend preseason high school summer leagues and pre and post season showcases as well. I try to read as much about players I can on the Internet as well. The Internet has been a very useful resource. There are so many sites that give updates on players, and they usually cover all showcases, summer leagues, and summer camps. I don't pay too much attention to the evaluations, I just look for basic information on kids. Also, I will follow-up w/ different contacts I have as well (high school coaches, aau coaches etc...). Kids should go to many camps, showcases and play in high school summer leagues. With the camps its important for kids to find out if they are going to camps where coaches will be and if they are going to camps during the NCAA evaluation periods. Kids will end up going to camps where there will be no college coaches attending or during a week where coaches are not allowed to evaluate. For the big time DI schools everything is different. From the travel (including Europe), to the selection of prospects, these schools all know the top 50-100 kids across the country because all these same kids will appear and compete at the same camps, showcases, and AAU tournaments. The big summer camps are the ABCD addidas camp in Teanack, NJ (special invite only) and the NIKE summer camp (Invite only). AAU is so popular right now due to the money that can be made by coaches and tournament directors and sponsors. All the schools will attend every major AAU tournament, and they subscribe to every major recruiting Internet publication that will provide them with frequent info and updates.

- Mike Donnelly, Head Men's Basketball Coach, Post University

FOR MORE INFORMATION

Appendix:
For a list on which schools offer which sports, please visit:
www.mazzmarketing.com or www.ncaa.org

Quantity Sales:
To buy reduced rate books in quantity, email wmazz22@aol.com

Seminar/Press
For more information on appearances and seminars, email wmazz22@aol.com

Additional Books
For other resources on the recruiting process, visit www.mazzmarketing.com

Baseball Athletes and Parents
Additional Baseball Information can be found on www.mazzmarketing.com

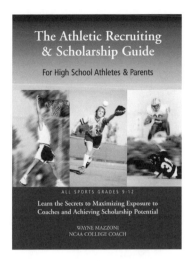

ORDER FORM

To order additional copies of *The Athletic Recruiting & Scholarship Guide,* simply fill out an order form below and mail to:

Mazz Marketing, Inc.
287 Courtland Avenue
Black Rock, CT 06605

Please send me *The Athletic Recruiting & Scholarship Guide.*

Number of copies: _____ x $19.95 (1 copy) = $_____

_____ x $17.95 (2-10 copies) = $_____

_____ x $15.95 (11-19 copies) = $_____

_____ x $13.95 (20+ copies) = $_____

☐ **Check enclosed** $_____

For Credit Card orders, please visit: www.mazzmarketing.com

Please send me *The Athletic Recruiting & Scholarship Guide.*

Number of copies: _____ x $19.95 (1 copy) = $_____

_____ x $17.95 (2-10 copies) = $_____

_____ x $15.95 (11-19 copies) = $_____

_____ x $13.95 (20+ copies) = $_____

☐ **Check enclosed** $_____

For Credit Card orders, please visit: www.mazzmarketing.com

Articles Published by Wayne Mazzoni

"College Should Play Fall Baseball," NCAA News

"Left-handed Pick Off Move," Scholastic Coach

"Signals," ABCA Coaches Digest

"What Level is Right for You," School Sports

"Pitching to Location," Junior Baseball

"Heads Up: Pitching is dangerous business," Baseball Digest

"How to Teach the Change up," Scholastic Coach

"What Makes Greg Maddux So Good," Scholastic Coach

"1st and 3rd Defense," ABCA Coaches Digest

"Gonzo Morning," Men's Fitness

"Give Knoblauch a Break," New York Times

"Time to Share the Wealth," New York Times

"Strike Zone," Connecticut Post

"Bonilla & Henderson," Newsday

"How Pitching Coaches Call Pitches," Scholastic Coach and Athletic Director

"How To Choose The Right Athletic Level," Sporting Scene, School Sports, All-Stater Sports

Other Books and Video's By Wayne Mazzoni

Books:
- You vs. You: Sport Psychology for Life
- The Left-Handed Pick-Off Move

Videos:
- The Left-Handed Pick Off Move
- The Athletic Recruiting and Scholarship Seminar

Also Available:
Quantity Book Discounts
Book on Audio Tape and CD
Seminar Video Tape
High School Seminar Booking (Over 150 schools to date)
Phone consultations

For more information visit: **www.mazzmarketing.com**

About the Author

WAYNE MAZZONI has been the head baseball coach at Post University (CT) since 1999. Prior to that he was an assistant at Fairfield University (CT) and Nova Southeastern University (FL). Mazzoni, from Northport, Long Island, is a 1991 graduate of Gettysburg College where he played baseball and received a BA in economics. He has a master's degree in Sports Administration from St. Thomas University (FL). Mazzoni has done internships in the baseball operations department for both the Buffalo Bisons (AAA) and Cleveland Indians. Coach Mazzoni has published many articles on baseball and recruiting and is also the author of several books and video projects, *The Athletic Recruiting and Scholarship Guide, 101 Motivational Tips, Left-Handed Pick Off Move, You vs. You: Sports Psychology for Life,* and *500 Tips for High School and College Athletes* and has appeared on Fox, ABC, News 12, and WFAN Sports Radio 660, among many others. He had spoken at over 200 high schools on recruiting and was a presenter at the ABCA National Convention and the World Baseball Coaches Clinic. Mazzoni and wife Keli live in Black Rock, CT, and have two boys, Colby and Brayden.

.